THE BARN CAME FIRST

Pearl

by
PEARL
SWIGGUM

Pearl Swiggum's first book was Stump Ridge Farm, published in 1990.

Pearl was born in 1914 in the village of Towerville, Wis. Her parents, Sigurd and Goldie Stevenson, had a large family and ran a general store there. She married Tillmen "Punk" Swiggum in 1934 and they had three children. In 1958 she began writing a column for the local newspaper, chronicling her experiences growing up and running a dairy farm for many years. This book is a compilation of many of those columns.

Photos: Front cover photo by daughter Marjie Jurgensen, back cover by granddaughter Kristi Deaver, others by the author, the scientific son-in-law Wayne Jurgensen, friend Royce Jones and niece Bonnie Olson.

Copyright© 1995 Pearl Swiggum
Published by
Stump Ridge Books
and Achenbach Printing, Boscobel, Wisconsin.
Printed by Straus Printing Company, Madison, Wisconsin

To order copies of this book, send $10 for each book to Stump Ridge Books, P.O. Box 187, Gays Mills, WI 54631-0187.

Personal notes may be mailed to Pearl Swiggum, Stump Ridge Farm, Route 4, Box 208, Viroqua, WI 54665.

ISBN 0-9646609-0-3 9.48

In Memory of Tillmen J. Swiggum
"Punk — T.J. — The Boss"

A favorite occupation of TJ—entertaining with his accordian.

FORWARD

From Stump Ridge to Stump Ridge is the simplified story of our almost 51 years together. As soon as we married we began renting Uncle Carl Stevenson's farm here on the hill. That only lasted one year. Married status gave me the courage to challenge his lifelong misogyny. He got along fine with Punk, who conceded that he was ruler of the farm. I could not tolerate him ruling the house and me.

After one year we moved to Towerville, the village where I was born, and lived in Grandfather Ole Stevenson's old home. For two years Punk worked on township roads, then with the renting of another uncle's valley farm we were back to the life I loved.

Vivid memories remain of those years. World War II and saying good-bye to all the young men in both families; of son Jim being born (both girls preceded him) and his father waking my sister and her husband by pounding on their door at five in the morning yelling, "I've got a boy."

Memories of us milking cows by hand and me running to the house between each cow to peek in the window and make sure the little ones were alright; of seeing Dorothy shaking the baby's bassinet and singing; of me whipping daughter Marjie, three years old at the time.

In the following pages are excerpts from 36 years of columns, some of them flashbacks to our earliest years, most about our daily life. A few parts did not appear in any column but are needed to advance the story.

This book is called The Barn Came First. Every farm woman knows that and as Punk often said, "Take care of the cattle and they will take care of you." I must have agreed for it was I who went to the barn in the middle of a twenty below zero night to check the water pipes or a cow due to freshen. None of it was a hardship. It was my pleasure.

The Years on Conway Creek

The pasture of the valley farm was dissected by Conway Creek. All year round it provided drinking water for our small dairy herd. During one long, hot summer it gave our family pleasure and late evening relief so that we would get to sleep on sweltering nights.

Fed by springs, its entire length, the creek had rapids, trout holes and just across from the house one fairly deep place with a sloping, sandy edge and a high bank on the side toward the house. After we finished the evening chores I took the girls, while their baby brother slept, across the creek and let them play in the sand.

One evening their father came walking across the pasture fully clothed, old black felt hat on his head, pipe in his mouth. We watched. As he neared the high creek bank the girls whispered, "Daddy isn't looking where he is going." He wasn't. They held their breaths, fearing that he would fall in. He did. Water splashed all over us and they screamed in terror.

Father with first born

But when he came up laughing they squealed with delight.

I was no swimmer but he was and better yet, he was a floater. He played the part of a raft and holding first one child, then the other on his chest, he floated up and down the swimming hole. After that, each evening when I took them to the creek they hoped he would come to join us and fall in just as he had the first time. But a creek can be a fatal attraction. I was always busy with housework, fieldwork, doing the laundry on a washboard. One day the girls were outdoors with a couple of my kitchen spoons making mud pies while I kneaded bread on the work table by the window where I could watch them. Suddenly Marjie was missing and I washed my hands to go looking for her.

Her tiny figure was out in the pasture headed for the creek and I ran. When I reached her I snatched her up and all the way back I repeated, "No, no, you must not go to the creek alone." But she did and was quite near the deep hole before I saw her.

As I jumped the cow pen fence I grabbed a small leafy branch

1

from a bush. Reaching Marjie, I turned her around, switched her bare legs with my twig and started her back to the farm yard saying all the way, "No, no." She cried and begged me to carry her but I refused. She never again went toward the creek alone.

―⁂―

A Delco Light Plant

There was no electricity in the country then but when the light plant had charged up the batteries, its smoke seeping up through the floor and around the outside cellar door, we could listen to his favorite program, a Chicago Cubs game, my favorite, the Shadow, and both our favorites, Tennessee Ernie Ford and his peapickers and WLS National Barn Dance.

―⁂―

Moving Day

Most young farm couples rented farms in the '30s and early '40s and many moved every year. March 1 was all we ever needed to know of trials and troubles and the year we bought Punk's home farm I had more than my share. There was deep mud in the road, snow everywhere else. The children were well but I had chills and fever and a sore throat. In a haze of misery I supervised taking down the beds, emptying cupboards, sending wagon load after wagon load of furniture and belongings to our new home.

There a fire had been built in the kitchen range, the first thing moved, and a sketchy meal thrown together for family and good neighbors. There was enough to do in the house, putting away, setting up beds and making them that a wife could not take part in driving the cattle (trucking didn't come until many years later) to an unfamiliar barn and getting them all into stanchions. So I have no memories of that. But the first night I will never forget. The girls were old enough to be excited about moving. Jim, a year and a half old, overwhelmed by strangeness, was inconsolable. He cried through the whole day and into night. Exhausted, I took him into bed with us and held him in my arms until we both fell asleep.

―⁂―

He Taught Me Everything I Knew About Farming

He taught me how to strip a cow dry, that when driving the team pulling the drag that I must not turn sharply at the end of the field, that the sound of a baby crying back in the woods was just a

2

rabbit communicating with another rabbit, how to tie a grain sack knot, how to plant, hoe, cut, pile, spear, haul, hang, take down and strip tobacco (the only job I hated was picking worms) and he tried but I just couldn't master spreading manure on a windy day.

The beauty and grandeur of nature are there for all to see but viewpoints may vary widely. A small child will enjoy them best from the middle of a mud puddle.

Hooray for The REA

Electricity came to rural areas while we rented Uncle Elmer's farm but he refused to have his buildings wired for it as every other owner in the country was doing. I asked why and he said, "All these newfangled things are bad. We would be better off if women were still cooking in a fireplace. You will see—now that electricity is here some woman won't be satisfied with just lights, she will get a stove and a refrigerator and then all her neighbors will want them too." He was right.

It was many years later that milking machines were introduced so farmers and their wives and families milked by hand. We had a custom I liked. During the summer we milked outdoors in a pen. It was much cooler and we could watch the countryside, birds, people going by. But as agreeable as the job was I developed a positive hate for Guernseys, one in particular.

One day I suppose I was more watchful of the kids playing outside the pen than I was of the cows. Every herd had a bunting order and the then dominant Guernsey rammed my cow on my blind side. Mine leaped half over me to get away. I went down, pail, milk and stool flying and one of the two cows stepped on my foot. That year I was glad to see autumn come with indoor milking.

There is an infallible way to become instantly beautiful. I walked into a neighbor's field of tobacco lying flat and began to pile. Someone yelled "You're beautiful."

A Gully Washer

What is a Crawford county four-inch rain?

It's the anguish in the eyes of a farmer as floods race over freshly planted fields; it is a blackbird singing on a cattail bobbing in the boiling chocolate; a heifer trying to find a clean drink and bolting in fright as a floating log bumps her knees; a century-old oak slowly tipping into the stream as its roots are undermined; little boys and puppies splashing in puddles. It is a gravel dune drifted across a pasture and a freshly gutted gully.

It is a herd of cows stranded on a hillside and a roundabout trek through wet weeds to milk out the heaviest producers; it is milk stools and salt box floating down the valley; creosote running down a wall from a soaked chimney; it is a county grader in the stormy dusk, blinking warning lights as it cleans gully debris off the highway; it is a frog on the left side of the road hopping across to what it thinks will be a better place to live while right hand frog hops left.

And the day after the sun comes out from behind dark clouds and shines alike on the mud of a little girl's pies and the mud that covers fields and pastures.

Then there were two—baby Marjie, Dorothy and Dad

⊸※⊶

Way back in my earliest days of newspaper writing I tried poetry and won an award which entitled me to ask published poets for advice. I got it: "Find someone to support you."

⊸※⊶

Delightful Dictionary

I have a most delightful dictionary. None of the last dozen words I have looked up are in it but I never close it dissatisfied.

To give you a for instance, "nostalgia" was not in it but near where it should have been was "note" as in music. And in the text was an illustration. There was a note with four little squiggles hanging from it like flags in a slight breeze and it was called a hemidemisemiquaver.

I defy you to call that dictionary search wasted. Now I know what fat opera singers were doing when we kids thought someone was standing behind them patting them on the back to make their voices quiver as they sang mightily. Hemidemisemiquavering was what they were doing.

A thought while gargling—it's time to wash the ceiling.

Kidspeak

Surrounded as I usually was by children—my own, nieces and nephews, then grandchildren—I was often entertained by their unintentional wit and their quips became a regular part of my columns.

One little girl munched on carrots and celery from the restaurant's relish tray, then sighed and said, "I guess they give you this stuff to keep you busy until the food comes."

Get down, puppy, your hands are dirty.

Hey, Grandma, I got the scales out, come pound me.

I fell down 'cause my skis went so fast they didn't wait for me.

I really wasn't lost. I knew where I was all the time.

How do they dye baby chicks for Easter? Dunk them by their feet and say "Hold your breath?"

Boy, look at my dog go. He's no slowpoke. He's a fastpoke.

What's in my berries? Oh well, he's dead.

5

Summer Pasture

We knew before we bought the home farm that it was two separate pieces of land. Being the farm where he grew up, of course we knew it. There was our base, 80 acres with the buildings and a richly flowing spring along the road across the narrow valley. It gushed into a big stock tank where teams stopped to drink in horse and buggy days.

Since there was no well on the farm we hauled our water from the spring to the house in ten-gallon milk cans for drinking, cooking, bathing, laundry. After we could afford to drill a well the stock tank was where we cooled the night's milking for hauling to the cheese factory in the morning.

Sixty acres, which everyone called the meadow, was almost a mile away and it was our custom, as it had been his family's, to alternate pastures, home and meadow all summer. They stayed in one for two weeks, then were moved to the other. The first move to the meadow in the spring was an adventure. Young heifers who had never been there livened up the jaunt.

Getting them through Star Valley was the tricky part of the trip. Luckily, half the people who lived there stepped outdoors when they saw the lead cow, a calm old matron, coming. The herd had three choices which made it tricky for those of us behind them. But there were enough volunteers to steer them all the one way they should go.

Milking there, by hand of course, became much more pleasant one summer. The cow pen where they were confined during milking had been out in the sun and if the cow we happened to milk was aimed in the wrong direction she didn't shade her milker.

But the fence had fallen down one summer and since Punk had to rebuild it anyway he moved it to an area where it encircled three trees. All the cows preferred the shade so it was pleasant for us milkers too, even if it was a little crowded.

Cows like to scratch themselves if there is anything to rub against and one of those three trees was ideal. It stood by an indentation in the pasture where the creek had flowed long before our time. Floods were frequent and changed the course of the creek often. There were three burls on the trunk of that tree, marking places where flood trash, maybe floating logs, had struck and bruised the tree. They made a great scratcher.

Having read how dairy herds in Norway were driven up to high pastures for the summers, then brought home again in the fall, I liked that arrangement and felt that we were carrying on a tradition of our ancestors.

Happiness, to a farmer, is having hay enough to last all winter, all new kittens being males and all new calves heifers.

Eating Raspberries

There are several ways to eat raspberries and now that the berry season is here it might be well to review them. As you know raspberries, unlike the spherical blackberries and strawberries, have a built-in fall-out shelter for insects.

The simplest method of course is to bump the bowl of berries or turn them over unobtrusively with a spoon while making polite conversation and keeping your listener transfixed. An occasional quick glance down will suffice to make sure no bug catches a ride to your mouth on a berry.

There are two variations of the cream method of detection. A direct approach is to pour on cream, skim off swimmers and eat. In the delayed drowning method there is a short pause after the cream has brought strong swimmers to the surface and they have been spooned out of the bowl. During the pause any bug or worm trapped under a berry will drown and a slight shake of the bowl will bring him floating to the surface.

Eye glasses should be kept on of course except by the blindly trusting who can probably enjoy a bowl of berries better with the glasses off. Then there is the method favored by the young involving facing the berries still on the bush, a clenched fist and a wide open mouth.

However you decide to eat berries, if you are able to at this point, you may take comfort from the fact that most food faddists agree on one thing, that we all need more protein but from other sources than red meat.

Words have different meanings for different people. To a farmer the word "danger" means walking behind a coughing cow.

A Job—With Pay

Somebody said, "Land sakes, why would you want to get a job in town, with all the milking and tobacco almost year around and all the other chores, don't you have enough to do?" So I explained to her that it is that "little money of my own" thing.

Not that I have a penny pinching husband but when I spend

our money sometimes I feel guilty. Spending my own money I won't. Few farm women, in fact few wives work outside their homes. There has always been told of almost every community that there was one husband who, when asked by his wife for some money to go shopping, exclaimed, "What did you do with the dollar I gave you last week?"

It isn't as if I would go to the city for a 40-hour week. It is just three days a week at the Crawford County Independent in Gays Mills and learning how to be a better writer from the editor Glenn Hagar. It is that the house is emptying—the girls are gone and Jim soon will be and I am feeling wings sprouting.

Punk has bought me a first class camera, Jens Fuhr has helped me equip a dark room and taught me developing pictures. You might say these things are feathers in my wings.

Part of learning to write is this column. When the boss (the one at the Independent, not the one at home) said "Write a column," I said "What's a column?" He explained that mine can be about anything I please. Fun writing. And getting paid for it.

Mud was their biggest attraction

This is the time of year to watch geese fly south, put on storm windows, find hubby's hunting coat, shotgun shells, hip boots, and re-new my griping license.

You would be surprised at how many wanted to take part in my physical fitness week. But you wouldn't be surprised that when I told them it was a week's work of harvesting tobacco they quickly backed down.

Calf Kindergarten

Most of the calves we are raising this year have been quick to learn how to drink from a pail but Fanny, the smallest, put up the biggest battle. Her hunger strike lasted two days and while that may not be long for an obese individual on a diet it is a long time for a new calf with no store of fat.

She wouldn't even swallow but her voice didn't lose strength and I couldn't stand her bawling so several times I filled a bottle of warm milk and simply poured it down her. Half of it went on the floor but enough went down her to stave off starvation.

For details I backed her into a corner, pried her mouth open and poured. She backed me out of the corner, all four legs flying. So I flopped her down on the straw and practically sat on her. The next day I brought her milk in a pail, stuck a finger in her mouth to pry it open, shoved her face down into the milk and said, "Drink or drown." She drank. And I'm beginning to understand why you don't see many fat farmers. We get such good exercise.

Here I am, back in the office after romping across 17 acres of tobacco dragging an ax, spear, jack, lath numbering in five figures, a slight touch of rheumatism, severe blisters and a sunburned nose. I put in about 50 bents of tobacco. With a little help.

Remember?

Remember when a pinch of cinnamon on a hot cookstove lid was the only air freshener and when you had buckwheat pancakes "going" all winter?

Remember when come spring you had to take sulfur and molasses to purify your blood because after all that buckwheat you needed it to prevent boils?

A cistern pump at the kitchen sink was a luxury, in fact any sink at all was a luxury, and a slop pail under it was a necessity? When saleratus biscuits always went with chicken and the extra biscuits, with homemade brown sugar syrup, was dessert?

When you butchered a hog at the start of winter, with the help

9

of neighbors, ground some meat into sausage, fried it and buried it in its own grease in a stone jar and in another stone jar you buried fried side pork; you cut up what would have been roasts and chops into small pieces and canned them in fruit jars in the oven; you rendered the lard, made head cheese and put hams, some of the side pork and all the bones in brine?

And those who could contrived outdoor storage places where some roasts and chops could be kept frozen all winter so you could have fresh meat like town people?

Remember what you had to do when the pump froze—carry a teakettle of boiling water out and pour it down alongside the sucker rod until the pump handle would work? And how the cistern pump had to sometimes be primed to get water to flow, probably because the leather was dried out and didn't fit tightly in the casing?

When you had a rule that you put off opening any of your hundreds of jars of fruit and vegetables until after Thanksgiving in hopes they would last through the winter?

When absolutely every meal but breakfast ended with dessert— if not sauce, then bread or cornstarch pudding? And every set of dishes included berry dishes?

When storm windows were unheard of and the children used the heavily frosted glass panes for drawing boards? You do remember all those things? Then I know about how old you are.

Wet Heaven

A shower after a long dry spell brings out the glee in all creatures. When we got that welcome rain after a month of combustible grass, combustible hay, combustible air, I looked out and every puddle had a robin in it. Makes a drouth, provided it isn't too long, almost worthwhile.

Look Ma, No Punctuation

I was washing my hair at the time and had shampoo in my eyes and he said whats in the refrigerator that I could have for lunch and what he was doing was rummaging for something to go with his mid-morning coffee a rotten Norwegian habit that I can't complain about too much because I always want mine too and I could hear dishes rattle and paper rustle but my memory is poor for leftovers so I said what does it look like and he said well theres something brown in a bread wrapper and something gray in a plastic bag and under a dish turned upside down on a plate theres what looks like an old pork chop and for gosh sakes what all have you got stuck away in here anyway and how long has it been here and dont you ever clean the refrigerator so I said with dignity before you criticize me you might look inside a couple of containers I didn't put in there and I know women who wouldnt allow them in their refrigerators I mean like what you call mousies only I think that is French for something you might find under a decayed board and until I get out from under all this soap my advice is if what you are looking at moves dont eat it.

Who Is Boss, Anyway?

A fellow columnist refers to her husband as The Better Half because "I don't dare call him The Boss like Pearl does because it might go to his head." Well, girl, what do you think calling him a better half does? My theory is that we might as well call a husband the boss. It certainly makes him happy and it deludes him into thinking he really is.

Oh Yes A Cow Can

Desk farmers claim a cow can't kick backwards. Actually, if a cow is startled she can belt away in so many different directions she seems as leggy as a skittish centipede.

I sat milking one of our leggier bossies one night, finished, picked up my stool and the pail, stepped across the gutter and slipped. A sideways clip with one hoof caught the pail and clanged it against my shin. Wow, that hurt.

Now when a cow gets upset and starts kicking she doesn't let one larrup do, she keeps clouting away until she is ready to settle down. So she caught me a wallop on one arm as I tried to keep from diving across the walk and into the other gutter. That sent me sprawling and upset the cows on the other side.

A big Guernsey clipped my ear and through the ringing in my head I could hear the swish of flying hooves of all the nearby cows. The only safe place (not clean but safe) was the middle of the walk so I sat there waiting for my rubber legs to re-starch and wept while I dug manure out of my ear. There is absolutely no direction that a cow can't kick. And I was glad none of the non-farming members of the family, who is everybody but me, were there to demand, "Now how can you say you love farming?"

Contoured Hillsides

Back when I was a kid farmers didn't have the lush, improved pastures they do now and our farmers around Towerville pastured the hillsides. I'm sure it was hard on the hill but it was great for us. Where cows grazed grass was short, there was no brush, not even trees and the surface was worn into parallel paths where they walked. Sometimes only a couple of feet apart, they gave the whole hillside the appearance of being terraced from top to bottom.

When the cows were somewhere else we scampered up and down, jumping from one well-worn path to another like two-legged mountain goats. One of the things I plan to do "someday" is find out if those parallel paths are still there hidden by grass long ungrazed and brush.

We kids were told that Wisconsin cows were short-legged on one side for grazing on our hillsides but we knew better. We were there and we knew they had cut the hillsides down to fit four equal length legs.

Jim joined his sisters at play

12

Ouch—Itch

Why did bedbugs disappear? When I was a child the pesky little parasites were only whispered about but they were around. Seems like they were most common in farm homes that saw different renters each March 1, causing the had nots to believe that the hads took them along everywhere they moved.

We owned our own home across the road from Towerville store and never moved so I never saw a bedbug until I went to town to work for my room and board and go to high school. Then I asked what that crawly thing was and was told "Sh."

I always thought my feet itched at night because I was too warm. When I reported this strange thing on a rare weekend home all my clothes were quickly dumped into boiling water. Strange behavior. When I asked why I was told "Sh."

When homes are closed tightly for the winter some women feel the need to purchase air fresheners to prevent a stale odor. For me there is nothing that improves the air quality as the scent of bread baking.

One of our cows was sick last week. After a visit from the vet and several days of sad-eyed illness she died. Now we have some veal calves ready to market. And through my mind runs two lines from a book of verse De Soto's Cecile Stury sent me: With this aching reverence for life I shouldn't be a farmer's wife.

Likely Labels

The narrow valley running past this farm was named Booger Gut. Don't bother to look at a map unless you have a township atlas because the name may not be there. But I haven't the slightest doubt early settlers named it that because my Aunt Ollie told me and she knew and remembered everything.

A graphic imagination tells me those early settlers, after imbibing too freely of the local home brew, probably suffered from a severe case of crazy mixed up intestines. Any arguments?

Near our home in Towerville there was a collection of rocks high on a hillside, a fearsome place to pass as we walked down to Star Valley Store with the pennies Dad gave us to go shopping in a different store. Looming over us, it was called Devil's Cave.

One sunny day we took our lives in our hands and climbed the hill to explore. Probably on the way home, fortified with candy. There

13

was nothing but rocks. No opening at all. Maybe that was how it got that name. Even the devil himself (and we loved to say that word when we had the right to because it was its name and everyone grownup did) couldn't get in. Nor out. So much for kids' fears and curiosities.

⸻

Four Seasons Country—The First

Spring comes on little webbed feet, timid and tardy. Peeking through a snow-laden cloud she sets a cardinal to reminding a winter-weary world that there is some cheer and unless the calendar is askew there will be more. But then spring and the cardinal go away to hide and the world continues to slog through drifts, to shovel, sweep and salt.

Comes March and such a mixed bag of weather that people chasing hats and pumping out basements and watching struggling crocuses almost wish for a return to straight, honest winter. Except for a day or two when spring touches a shoulder that happens to be pointing south and off comes a coat.

Spring surfs down water-filled roadsides, dry runs suddenly splash full with the collection of streams coming from snowdrifts up in hillsides, then overnight spring reaches the creek and is frozen in. Ducks waddle away to the warmth of the barn or hunt for open water of a spring coming directly out of a crevice in a hill.

But there comes a night when thunder rolls and lightning threatens every tall tree and a long gone memory stirs of someone saying, "It takes a good thunderstorm to break up the frost in the ground." That must be true because this morning grass that looked dead yesterday shows a hint of green and crocuses have made a comeback.

In Wisconsin spring has many setbacks but like any other lady who gets an idea into her head, she can't be stopped.

⸻

Ego Alteration

April has its troubles with split personality: a little of March still in its makeup, a little of May sneaking in as a set-up for disillusionment when March creeps back. A spatter of rain turns to a flurry of snow, hiding the crocuses and snowdrops, the muck of the swamps where there must be three more freeze-ups before winter finally lets go. Winter hates to. And sometimes in fury it throws a straitjacket around April's pastel finery trying grimly to maintain the status quo. No season is so stubborn.

14

The first month of winter was a sight to be seen,
Blazoned all over with bright red and green.
January arrived in whistling white,
February's ice was crackling bright.
Then March blew in with things going thud
And the color of March is mud.

A House Too Small

Comes that time of year that puts the greatest strain on farm marriages. March—the month of indecision. For him: do I clean out the hay shed tomorrow or will it be too cold; can I begin to haul manure out on the fields again or will I get stuck? For her: do I dare take the mattresses out to air, throw away his hunting and fishing regulations, old football schedules and deer tags?

She has to hear weather reports five times before daylight; he has to hear how much she could get done if only the weather were better. She wishes he would spend more time in the barn, he wishes she would spend less time between him and the television set. With high hopes on a sunny day she gets him all packed to go fishing—then it starts snowing.

Barn jackets, boots and patience are wearing thin. The calendar says we are nearing the end of winter and we will soon be outdoors, working longer and healthier days. And through chills and chilblains, sneezes and sniffles a lawn mowing session on a blistering July day looks wonderful in retrospect and anticipation.

Togetherness sounds great in stories. Congenial, convivial, close association; side by side through thick and thin, 24 hours a day after day. Lovely in early December, by the end of a long, hard winter the togetherness of two housebound people is like two cats in a gunny sack.

There is nothing quite so effective for clearing up lingering nasal congestion from an old winter cold as having the family dog tangle with a skunk just off the back porch.

Footloose And Fancy Free

Spring passed this way one day and I followed her. Down the road that slopes toward the sun I followed, reaching for her shimmering robe as she skipped from side to side, her warm feet leaving indentations in the honeycombed icy banks of sparkling rivulets.

She bounded over a dirty snowdrift dam, skipped along bruising not one crocus with her sunshine slippers, leaped high to stroke a shaggy pussywillow, then bent low and uncurled a fern frond's self-clutching fingers. Just as she and the rivulet the ice-rimmed open creek I reached to grasp her calling "Stay."

There was a sound above and I shivered to see snow swirling over the crest of the ridge pushed fast by a howling north wind. I turned and spring was gone. But she will venture back and I will be ready, a trap baited with lure made from scent of flower, croak of frog and swish of bluebird wing. Then she will have to stay for good. And I want credit.

Jim joined his sisters at play

What Sort of Man Was He?

Punk was a Norwegian of few words, fewer humorous acts and even fewer compliments, every one well worth remembering.

One noon around the table were a half-dozen youngsters, nieces and nephews often joined our own brood. Later there were grandchidren. That day I made pancakes, which suited everyone.

As they ate Punk poured a lot of syrup on his pancake, cut it up, then asked, "She sure makes light pancakes, doesn't she?" All agreed. Then he jumped up and said, "What's that going by?" Of course all the kids left the table to look out doors or windows. He stuck a piece of pancake to the ceiling and sat down.

When they came back, disgruntled because they had seen nothing, he pointed upward at the proof of my pancakes' lightness. Some may have doubted but all thought it very funny. I had to clean off the sticky syrup.

No talker, he, except maybe down at the crossroads store with his farmer friends. Certainly never to me about anything that involved "feelings." Or almost never.

One day after Jim had graduated from high school and left home and the visiting nephew moved in saying, "You need me now," we sat silently at our morning coffee. He must have worried over his problem for days, maybe weeks, trying to find the words to tell me.

Suddenly he blurted it out, breaking our long silence and startling me: "Sanford doesn't like me." I reacted with shock: "How can you say such a thing? I know he not only likes you, he respects and admires you, that's why he is here. What ever makes you think that?"

"He never talks to me," he said.

I thought for a minute, then asked, "Do you talk to him?" He said, "Of course not. What could I talk to him about?"

I guess I was pretty exasperated because I said, "For gosh sakes, the weather, the crops, the cows, haying or fencing or whatever you are doing together, hunting, guns, fishing, the river, baseball, football." Out of breath I stopped. Silence.

Then my memory kicked in and I said, "Know something? You said exactly what you did just now, back when Jim was that age. Do you and Jim have trouble finding something to talk about?" I expected him to say, "Aw, you just made that up," but he sat silent for a time, then asked in a subdued voice, "I did?" set down his cup and went out. Often after that watching them, I could see there was good communication.

Compliments were few, yes, but so good. At the Conway Creek farm we did most of our field work alone. Couldn't afford to hire help. The girls were small and had to go to the field with us. I found some old carpeting and asked him to pound four fence posts into the ground at the end of the tobacco field. Then I stretched the carpeting across and nailed it to each post, making a shelter from the sun where theycould play with their toys while we worked. Looking down the field at them he said, "You sure are a good mother."

I was never known for good housekeeping and once my brood graduated from floor and lap babies to become runarounds I didn't scrub often. One morning after breakfast he went to the barn while I hurried with the dishes, then mopped the floor. Nice and shiny, my linoleum was.

Coffeetime arrived and so did he. Sitting down at the table, he bent over and brushed hay and chaff out of the cuffs of his overalls (he always bought them too long, then turned up the bottoms) and there the mess was, on my clean floor. Arms akimbo I said with a lot of sarcasm, "I like you because you're so neat."

He looked at the chaff, at me, picked up his coffee and thought a while, then said, "I like you because you're not."

All our lives I had done things that he disapproved of. I bought a pool table and he was angry. Said, "It won't go down the basement stairs," and that was about all he said for days. Before it was delivered the scientific son-in-law and Sanford came and removed the railings on both sides. Curiosity got him to the basement just before the descent began. After its installation and adjustment I could hardly get him to come up for supper. We played thousands of games over the years. He won most.

I was sneaky. Some things he disapproved of I got done while he was fishing all day. Like the floor register, or ceiling register, in the valley house. The uninsulated upstairs was cold in winter but he said a register was out of the question.

I secretly bought one and the minute he was gone fishing I rushed down to Star Valley to borrow a keyhole saw and some advice. It was neatly in place long before the evening milking. Nothing was said.

The last and greatest compliment came because of the sum of all the sneaky and disapproved of things I did. His health was failing that summer but he still enjoyed going to the Mississippi to fish. For the nine years of his retirement we did it a lot. That last summer I bought a small camper, secretly of course, then took him to look at it.

Without a word, but a sort of bemused expression, he studied it inside and out, sat on the seats which made into beds, looked in cupboards, refrigerator, stove oven and got back into the car. It was to be delivered next day.

Driving home I could stand it no longer. "Aren't you going to say something?" I asked. "Aren't you even going to yell? Are you mad?" What he said was, "Nothing you do surprises me anymore." That was all. We took it to the river five times before he said he could no longer make the trip. His pleasure was worth every cent I paid for it.

———

A local newspaper received a release from a college referring to the incoming class as "freshpersons." Where will it all end? I can guess. And that will be the day I secede from the huperson race.

Backroom Tricks

There have been some shenanigans going on lately in my office involving such tricks as my glasses taped to the desk top and the space bar of my typewriter taped to the carriage. One of these days some joker is going to hear a punch line right out of Gunsmoke—Pow.

The boys in the backroom have an aversion to my poetry, too, saying it is an awful waste of newspaper space. But when something terrific or traumatic happens in my life I just have to go Walt Whitman.

The end of World War II brought some changes. So did burned out grates and a hole in the wall of the cookstove oven clear through into the firebox. So we bought one of the first electric ranges off the once totally defense products assembly line and hauled the cookstove to the dump.

Walt is on the loose.

Kitchen Range

Antiquated monster with a grating smile,
Squat warmly there as we discuss a while
Your past, as rich in memories as cream is rich that's put to sour
In warming oven beside bread set and raising for an hour.
A thousand snowy mittens from generations grown have dried
Where cast-iron fretwork curlicues a shelf along the side.
Children warmed their clothes and dressed by open oven door.
There, babies bathed on mother's lap in water from the reservoir.
Kittens, piglets, chicks and pups knew you as foster mother.
Some, revived, returned to nests. Pets never knew another.
Though plans for modern decor show that I must part with you,
Going, you leave a four-foot space and take my kitchen's heart
   with you.

A boy becomes a man when he discovers there are ways to make a mark in life other than burning his tire tread into the highway.

A new way to tell time: Inform your baby sitter that you are leaving ten minutes before Have Gun—Will Travel and to have the children in bed by five minutes after Gunsmoke.

Busy Work

Punk bought a new pipe last week. I said, "Why are you buying another, your rack is full?" He explained that he had only six and besides three free packages of tobacco came with it.

A pipe-smoking philosopher claims that no major crime has

ever been committed by a pipe-smoker. Good reason. What with digging around in the bowl of a well-cured briar, filling with a favorite blend, tamping it just right, lighting, puffing, drawing, then lighting again, there just isn't time to commit a minor crime, let alone a major one.

Did He Like It?

It was certainly unplanned but might have been inevitable, a quirk of Fate, that when I got a job at the Crawford County Independent at Gays Mills in 1958 I would begin writing a column that would last longer than I expected to live.

Certainly it was characteristic of me to miss signs that husband Punk was silent on the subject. Awareness took several years and didn't come like a bolt from the blue. It was more like beginning to wonder why he didn't ever mention it. Maybe he disapproved?

One day after the mail had come and we sat with it over our morning coffee I burst out, as he held the Independent up between us, "You don't like my column, do you?" A man of few words, who had to have those few dragged out of him, he took a few more drinks, then said, "I liked one once. It was about fishing."

Never again did he comment on any of my subjects but through the years I was reassured of his approval, if not of a particular subject, at least of my writing. There was the time a man stopped me on the street and said, "You shouldn't be picking on your husband in your column. That's not nice." I reported to Punk and asked if I should. "No, no, don't quit," he said.

Then one day he came home from ice fishing to report, quite excitedly for him, that a man fishing from a hole in the ice beside him over on the Mississippi River, had asked, "Do you know that Swiggum woman who writes?" I'm sure that he was surprised, maybe even impressed, that any man who didn't have to and a sportsman at that, would read it.

From then on if I was sitting at the typewriter he put on his radio earphones so as not to bother me. Stifle my Muse? And if I didn't get at the Wednesday writing job he said, "Hadn't you better get in there and go to work?" Approval enough.

New mothers get baby-raising advice from two classes of people. Those who have had babies and those who haven't. And the latter, while they may be in the minority, are the most emphatic that they know best.

Summer is here and the milk cans, filled with the night's milking, are hauled over to the spring for cooling. That is the richly flowing spring that filled a stock tank for passing teams years ago. And where we stood the other day drinking during a break from tobacco work when a car stopped.

A man got out, a government employe of some kind from the insignia on the car, probably conservation related. He watched us drink then said, "I would rather drink poison." Shocked, we listened as he raved on about the chance that wild creatures might have died on the hill above.

He drove away and we went on drinking. The spring had been the source of all water used by Punk's family and of ours until we drilled a well near the house. Many people were in the habit of coming from town and filling jugs for their drinking water. Nobody could ever remember anyone being sick from drinking it. One man's poison is another man's nectar.

Television has come to the land, brought down off the hill from an antenna and through "railroad track" lines, all vulnerable to most any kind of storm. And the hero of the day is Gorgeous George.

One of our favorite neighbors is partnering us in a little barter and trade. We trade lard (we have seven gallons left from the two hogs we butchered last winter) for eggs. This farm hasn't known poultry since the old hen crowed last fall and we ate her. Would I lie?

Boys—Love 'em

The visiting nephew is a budding stand-up comic. Planting tobacco started last week and he was asked if he could plant in his canvas shoes. "Why not," he asked. "I don't plant with my feet."

Telling some bystanders he had been chased by a bull he was asked, "How old was it? About six months?" He snarled, "What was I supposed to do—stop and ask its age?"

The boys repaired the diving board in the pasture swimming hole just in time for it to turn too cold for them to make use of it. And a neighbor reported, "This is the first time I ever planted tobacco in a coat." That was 1961.

Nobody Dumps A Good Cow Dog

Completely useless, this dog ran in full grown one day and adopted us. Poor Pooch, surely a city dog, probably outgrew his cuteness and was dumped near a "they will keep him" farm. He put on a frantic pretense of courage when he saw his first cow.

Loyalty? He disliked and mistrusted everybody but family. If we had to call the doctor, before he came we put Pooch in the back bedroom with the door tightly closed. Once he barked desperately the whole time and after the doctor was gone I peeked in the door. He was leaping around on our bed challenging the dog doing the same thing in our dresser mirror.

Loyalty took him along with the kids picking berries or anything in the garden. He ate all the berries hanging low enough. In the garden he ate anything they were gathering. Favorite place in winter was sitting on a kitchen chair by the stove. Sometimes he snoozed, then jerked awake. Sometimes he snoozed and fell off the chair.

Future Farmer? No

One morning Punk came home from Star Valley. All the farmers around hauled their milk in ten-gallon cans to the cheese factory there, then went to the store for coffee and some gabbing. He announced that one older neighbor told him that it was time we must make our kids, not very old at the time, learn to milk cows.

Dorothy and Jim agreed that they were willing to learn. And they quickly did, easing our work a great deal. Marjie, who was usually quite docile, went stubborn: "I won't learn. I don't need to because I will never, never marry a farmer." And she didn't.

Among people I truly admire are those who say, "I wouldn't attempt to give you advice." And don't. And those who stand at your door ready to leave and say, "I must go now," and do.

Unfair—Unfair

Among unfair marriage practices is announcing early Saturday morning, just as I have made a tight, full schedule of catching up on long-neglected housework, "The cows are out." I wonder if the thousands of other farm wives who hear that get as quickly and fiercely angry as I do.

And I wonder why livestock can't schedule their breakouts for some other time than a sopping wet morning after an all night rain when you have just talked yourself into work you didn't want to do in the first place so was all ready to get it over with in a hurry.

But when we had located the cows and he went to let down a fence so we could drive them back into the pasture and I sloshed through knee-high hay to get around them and it began to rain again I didn't care because I was soaked anyway, and I realized this is a part of farming and it always will be. And I wouldn't have my life any other way

---

Nature's Eulogy

Uncle Carl Stevenson, an old bachelor living alone on his Stump Ridge farm, has died. Towering pine windbreak, replanted forests, lush legumes and grasses growing thickly on his conservation farmed acres are a living memorial to his lifetime of stewardship.

Winter's west wind dirge through the pines is muffled by the songs of returning birds. For a time they will make their homes, raise their young and return south without a human observer. And the farm will lie idle until the farm is sold.

Funny how . . . greeting cards say exactly what you want to, and sometimes better.

Frogs and caterpillars are never satisfied with where they live and must cross the road—right to left or left to right.

How much longer it takes flower seeds to push through the ground and get down to the growing business than weed and even vegetable seeds.

How that last sigh of my coffee percolator sounds like a young mother when she has finally gotten her boisterous babies to sleep.

Old Dogs Can't Learn

Our new tobacco planter certainly attracted a lot of attention. With the old as you growers know, Dorothy and I sat on seats almost dragging on the ground and facing front. And we dropped plants in the ground that way. When Mollie begins goofing off as she often does so that Cap has the whole load to pull—us, the water barrel with Punk up on the seat he slaps Mollie on the rear with the reins and we plant at a gallop. We are ready.

Now we plant facing backwards and Punk is pulling the planter with the tractor. A difference in the sound of the click and the constant question—which end is up as we place plants with the roots facing wrong to me, and having to work quickly before the fingers which grab the plant go by empty—all that proves to me the truth of that saying about old dogs and new tricks.

The most attentive audience during the whole five acres of planting was the three boys who climbed out of the swimming hole at the bend in the creek, draped themselves facing backward across the water barrel and offered criticism and advice. Can't say it helped much.

Good Eating

The visiting roosters, sent to the farm because they didn't turn out to be the cute pets that were expected, got it in the neck one day after they began tormenting the kittens. At least one did. There's an old saying "Never name anything you plan on eating." When we got mad Abner tasted great. I don't know about Lum, he went back to the investor.

Cow Tamer

The girls have been gone to jobs in Madison for a couple of years and now son Jim has left the farm and the visiting nephew is no longer visiting. After years of coming every weekend and joining in whatever work was in progress he came this time carrying his belongings and said "Now that Jim is gone you need me." We do. We two share chores— I get up in the morning and help milk, he helps milk in the evening.

One of best memories I will keep is after we had enlarged and modernized the barn, bought a milking machine partly financed by a small inheritance from Uncle Carl, and I stood in the middle of the barn between the rows of cows shaking, crying, "We'll never get these cows used to milkers. I'm going to get rid of them. Get out of there, Sanford, she will kill you."

A big Holstein had lifted one foot, pulled the milker loose from the strap and was jumping up and down on milker and strap and kicking in all directions with Sanford right beside her. I was bawling my head off. Sanford said, "You go to the house." I did.

Next milking time that Holstein was a changed cow. She stood still for the strap and milker as did every other cow in the barn. I came that close to spending the rest of my arthritic life milking cows by hand.

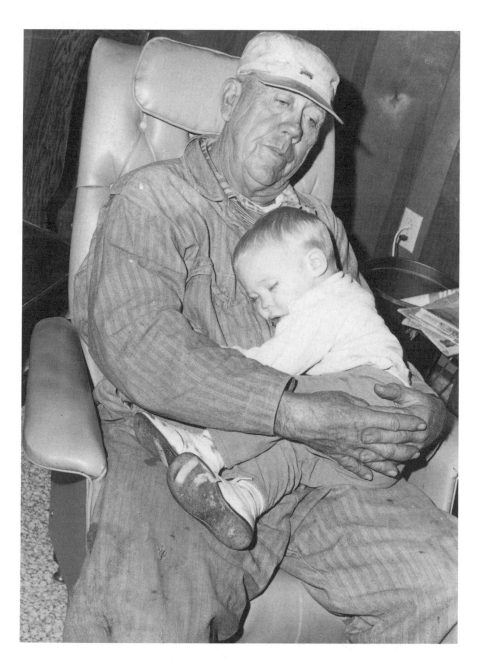

No better place to sleep for Alan than Grandpa's big lap.

Tobacco Harvest

The time is coming when we will begin harvesting tobacco and how sweet it is that the arrival of harvest coincides with the arrival of visiting nephews who were short and chubby last year, six-foot and sinewy this year. I think I will keep them for a while.

I have some new high class harvesting equipment. I preempted a brass-tipped spear the first day, keep it hidden, and after a sad experience with a round-handled axe I monogrammed one made from an old saw blade. That homemade one snicks off stalks at a touch and if I see anyone reach for it I scream, "That's mine."

I bought a box of apples for baking during harvest and got a sack of early Macs that the nephews put in the spring alongside the field to cool for lunching. The youngest asked what I was going to do with the others and I said I would make pies. He said, "I hope you make apple pies. They're my favorite." He is quite young.

⸻

As happy as:
a cow with a bale of second crop, no-rain alfalfa all to herself.
a chickadee with a freshly filled feeder.
a pup with a new bone, an old shoe or somebody's ankle.

⸻

Fish Feast

There may be some wives who resent their husbands going fishing. Not I. When mine announces in the morning that he is going and leaves the breakfast table to go dig angleworms I give a silent cheer.

It isn't just that a woman with a farmer husband rather than the kind that goes to work and punches a time clock is happy to get her man out so she can be alone for a while that she packs sandwiches, coffee— whee, I won't have to make dinner. It's also the anticipation of those crisp fried fish filets for supper.

I am so happy being a farmer's and a fisherman's wife that I carry on a project of my own, sort of aiding and abetting. Anyone with knowledge of earthworms knows they disappear if their living conditions are poor but grow and multiply if they are good. I make sure they are perfect.

With a family to cook for I make a lot of garbage in a day—all sorts of peelings and coffee grounds. Gourmet food for worms. The pail containing garbage is also filled with water. Emptied on the same spot every day, the shady side of a building, they become a ShangriLa for worms even during a drouth. So I send him off with a smile and greet him at day's end with a bigger smile.

I put up shelves where I need them and do other small carpentry jobs but some of my building projects look like I trained under Frank Lloyd Wrong.

Earthy Philosophy

Earthworm poked his head above ground and called "Greetings, Robin, I see you are early. I hope you have already dined on slugs and grubs and other creepy things because I would like to have a serious discussion with you. And a safe one, too. We do have much in common, I feel, you being, as that old saying about the early bird goes, the getter and me being the gettee.

In your travels south to north you may have noticed how much faster the world is spinning these days, east to west. Being above it, as it were, this should have impressed you. In fact I am surprised that you could start from Louisiana and heading straight north land in Wisconsin. Seems like you should get lost somewhere off the coast of Maine. Even here within the ground the pace fairly makes me dizzy.

"Our purpose here on earth and our ultimate destiny have been causing me deep thoughts (and you must admit, considering my habitat, that I am especially qualified for deep thought) and I must say with pardonable smugness that I am satisfied with both my purpose and destiny. The value of a life is measured by what it accomplishes in its three score and ten or in your case its approximately four, or in mine .75.

"You being one of the environmentalists' darlings can surely see that my fulfillment is double, providing as I do both provender for you and pleasure for that unique creature who would rather be sitting along a creek bank dangling me in the water than watching a ballet in Madison Square Gardens. Not being much of a traveler I'm not sure where they are held but it is the only fancy place that I can think of that I would care to visit. Gardens, you know.

"How dare I telescope my head (at least I think that's what this end is) up out of the ground and discuss destiny with you, my natural enemy? One of my grandmothers three generations back became involved with a night crawler and since then our clan has gone by the name of Speedy. You haven't got a chance of making me your lunch so straighten your head upon your neck and listen.

"You give much pleasure to humans, you help control unnameable insects and now and then, perish the thought, provide a meal for a hungry cat. Do you dig me? You have a worthwhile purpose in life.

Well so do I. And since we all must depart this earthly (get that term, from a worm) realm, let it be in a blaze of glory. Whoops—but I'm not ready.

⊂₩⊃ ·

I have a smart husband. As I clean the combination windows he says, "Good thing you know how to take them apart and get them back together again. I sure don't." Then he never stays around to learn how it's done. That's how smart he is. But why should I complain? I say and do the same thing when he is cleaning fish.

⊂₩⊃ ·

Cows and People

A city relative writes that her neighbors don't believe that farmers name their cows after their kinfolk. Shucks, we do it all the time. Fact is, we can't get down to the city to visit Aunt Maria and cousins Sarah and Julia. Have to stay home and keep an eye on Maria, Sarah and Julia so they don't break into the cornfield and eat themselves sick.

And speaking of Julia, I learned one milking time that some cows truly are almost human. In the small old barn there is little room for play space so a section of the walk behind the cows became the children's zone while we milked 16 to 18 cows by hand.

I returned from emptying a pail of milk into a ten-gallon can to see Julia, a huge brindle, backing across the gutter. Accidentally not tied, she was bent on getting out. I screamed one of those hopeless end-of-the-world cries and she froze with a foot in the air held over the little ones and stayed that way while I grabbed all three to safety. If there is a cow heaven I know Big Julia is there.

⊂₩⊃ ·

As spring weather goes March is a breach of promise, April a tentative proposal, May a vow kept, at least as well as most.

⊂₩⊃ ·

A test of marital harmony is putting up a tent when one performs on the follow-the-directions plan and the other plays by ear.

⊂₩⊃ ·

Time, my dears, will erase painful memories of that mistake you just made. So will the next mistake.

⊂₩⊃ ·

Calico Cats

Mustard and Oliver, our calico mother cats, are not husky but they make up in spirit what they lack in size. While they eat supper in

28

the barn they have had to contend with two of the neighbor's hounds which we, not knowing their names, have tagged Stupid and Sad Sack.

One night Sad Sack's internal clock must have told him it was milking time. He came across the valley, up through the pasture, under the fence and in the barn door. Flicking glances this way and that he walked slowly through the barn. Mustard let him get almost to the cats' dish, then she advanced. He stopped, gave ground and that began his Waterloo. She crowded the big hound the length of the barn, flicked out one paw, hooked him on the nose and he went crying back down the valley.

Spectacle Squabble

How come you keep insisting I wear my glasses to the barn I said just remember you don't need any and how often I miss the bottom step because the reading part makes me blind when I look down. Not only that no darn cow is going to flip them into the gutter if I leave them in the house or shove her hip into my face when I am putting the milker on her and maybe smash them into my nose. So there.

What you forget he said is that you have a hard time even seeing the barn without the distance part of the glasses and you have to grope your way through the chores. You have trouble recognizing the cows. Well I said if I squint real hard I can make them out and by feeling I know if I already milked one. Just push me in their general direction and I will do fine.

How come you never wear them outdoors then like when you are helping me load corn and oats there wouldn't be any danger of a cow knocking them off so why don't you? For your information, I said, finding the corncrib is the easiest thing I do. If the sun is shining the corn sort of glows and if it is a dark day I just aim myself due northwest and walk until I bump into the crib and he said oh I thought that you were worried the sun might wear them out and I said if there is anything I can't stand it's a sarcastic farmer.

In the wintertime they get all steamed up when I come in out of the cold and in the summertime they get all steamed up from sweating when I am working and I might as well be blind from not wearing them as from trying to look through steam. I hate glasses. Especially bifocals.

Foxed Focus

Getting used to bifocals
Is as hard as the devil.
The world has become,
Like the fashion in houses
split
LEVEL

Little Joe, the only farm cat to survive the distemper epidemic, is a true sportsman. Most of our mice jump out of feed sacks and safely reach shelter. He only catches what he can eat.

Winter 1960 and Little Joe

That was a real King Wenceslaus snowstorm last week. The snow certainly lay round about, deep and crisp and even. Spruce that we planted on the hillside above the dry wash are almost hidden. After the kittens recovered from their astonishment they went burrowing glee-fully, hunting through the snow for what, only kittens know.

Yes, we have more felines. The farm was just too catless with only Little Joe. But we did not take chances on their health and they had distemper shots. If only there was immunization against accidents. Spats is more reserved and quiet than Spike but he is accident-prone. He has already lost two of his lives, once by being stepped on by a cow, the second by being run over. There must be kitten angels. He wasn't hurt either time.

I brought home another kitten that was hanging around the Gays Mills Independent office and the little orphan of the storm is now playing with Spats and Spike and getting his face washed by foster-father Little Joe, who is good-hearted for an old tomcat.

Good-bye—Hello

I hate Good-byes. When I have to say it I do so quickly, then go. I love Hellos.

Have you ever thought of the difference in the two words? The one is upbeat, the other down. Hello is fresh, cheery, a word to be shouted; drab and dreary Good-bye—whispered.

Hello enlivens and invigorates. It fills the air with happiness and a rainy day with sunshine. Good-bye stings and burns. It's a word to say quickly and as quickly turn away from. Hello is bright, glowing, alive.

Good-bye is gray.

Good-bye is looking down a dark tunnel with no light at the end.

Good-bye is going to bed hungry and no hope for breakfast. It is turning the head to the pillow and wetting it with tears. Good-bye is a sore throat that reaches down to the heart.

Fashion—Forget It

The girls and I went browsing through a pattern and fabric de-partment in La Crosse while the Boss shopped elsewhere in a hardware store. I wasn't buying, not definitely, but if I had found linen in blue with a few white specks woven in here and there so kringla crumbs wouldn't show, plus a conservative dress pattern, I'd have bought.

I had read that the chemise had demised but there it was, stretched out from the shapeless waistline to a shapeless hemline and called a triangle.

Trapeze? The fashion designer who took the trapeze of a few months ago, combined it with the Empire and named it the Empire trapezerie is either sick, sick, sick or hates women.

The bubble? It would make a woman look like a full potato sack with legs. There might be some advantage in wearing one if you were a shoplifter looking for a man but I think the only male you would attract would be one in uniform, with star, handcuffs and billy club.

No—a blouson? Sure, if you were a shoplifter with no ambition. The bulge where the waist should be would only hold a few baubles and bangles and maybe a mink collar.

But that bubble. Inside the puckered bottom tent an ambitious female larcenist could put a diamond tiara, a mink stole—in this case a stole mink—and a galvanized tin washtub.

I went out of there shaking my head and muttering, a la Gertrude Stein, "A dress is a dress is a dress."

———

Daughter Marjie demanded a penny to weigh herself. She hopped on the machine, gasped, "That's a lie," and hopped off.

———

Never Never

Back when I was a kid there was one word we heard a lot, followed haphazardly by four more.

Never jump rope on a full stomach. It will upset your digestion and give you a stomach ache.

Never go swimming on a full stomach. You will get a cramp and drown.

Never play tag on a full stomach. You will get a stitch in your side.

Never go to bed on a full stomach. You will have nightmares.

Never try to study on a full stomach. Your blood is so involved with your digestion that your brain will be deprived and you will grow up stupid.

Trouble was, my stomach was always full.

———

Help

Will some other mother of a young football player help me? Tell me how to get their clothes clean. Jim brings home mud-crusted, grass-stained jersey and pants and says, "Whatever you do, don't shrink them."

Don't tell me to just set the washer for mild and toss 'em in. I don't have one. So far I have soaked them in the sink in lukewarm water with lots of soap and used a nylon brush. I am afraid they will take on a hand-washed look. So help.

Aren't We Nice?

Waiting in Madison's Rennebohm Drugstore for daughter Dorothy, who works there, I visited with the young French wife of an Air Force career man who is stationed at Truax Field. Confiding that she had only been in this country a short time, she said she had taken a job behind the fountain, worked one day and almost quit in frustration at trying to learn our language well enough to hold her job.

Urged by many to give it a longer try, she was glowingly grateful for customers' acceptance of her and to a man/woman their patience and willingness to help her learn. Listening to what her delightful accent did to our familiar words, I couldn't help but feel she was giving something back to us.

The Cow Pen Is A Stage

When we have the cows up on the meadow pasture and milk in the cow pen beside Tainter Creek we often have an audience of fishermen, picnickers and just plain fence-leaners.

Some of all categories were bystanding one night and one asked if two cows that resembled each other were sisters. "No," said the visiting nephew, a budding stand-up comic—in this case a sit down on a milk stool one—"they are grassmates."

There is no stronger hint at man's immortality than the first eye to wobbly-eye encounter with a new grandchild.

Happiness Is

old Laddie running around, chasing his tail and enjoying his second puppyhood.

buying clothes without trying them on and having them fit when you get home.

an income tax refund and learning to polka.

starting to work on icy roads and finding the scariest places sanded.

X-rays showing the insides are in even better condition than the outsides.

cardinals in the snow, a chickadee on the hand, two squirrels chasing each other through the oak, a child's voice: "Goodie, you did make sugar cookies."

Happiness is a two-way country lane.

Grandchildren—Yes

They are so much fun to buy things for but he thinks I overdo it and calls me a spendthrift. How can he say that when I am such a saver? For goodness sakes I still have in the fridge a bottle of Worcestershire sauce I bought back when I thought it was pronounced the way it looks. And way in the back of the fridge are covered bowls that have been there so long I have forgotten what is in them and I am afraid to look. That's saving.

We don't often have the grandchildren for weekends so when we do I have to dust off some old seldom used phrases: "Don't run down the stairs." "Don't try to walk up the basement stairs in your rollerskates." "Don't stand there and think with the refrigerator door open."

I used to take a magazine devoted to the health and well-being of the elderly but I had to drop it. There is a limit to the numbers of symptoms and cures that one body can absorb.

She said I like your column and I said I'll walk along with you so you can tell me more and then I said do you like it when I pick on my husband and she said oh my yes so now I have a real excuse. As if any wife needs one.

One of our regular visitors will be getting his sheepskin soon but I'm afraid his college knowledge won't take him very far on a farm. He is an agricultural moron. Wondering one day what my lame cow, who has the run of the farm, was doing I asked the college grad to check. He came back and reported, "She is OK—just sitting down by the corn-crib."

The valley farm where two generations of Swiggum children grew up.

New Adventure

One Sunday we walked the woods on Uncle Carl's farm up on Stump Ridge. It wasn't easy. He could never bear to cut a tree even if it should have been so we pushed through undergrowth and climbed over dead, downed trees. Some of the nephews went along and one got so far ahead he couldn't hear his old aunt's cautioning. When he came to a fence he climbed the four strands of barbed wire, intending to jump from the top strand.

The fence post broke and he dived backward, tangling with barbs on all four wires and landing on his head with his feet still skyward. A search showed a dozen rips in his clothes and three on himself.

Driving back to the valley I remarked that there certainly were a lot of people out riding and enjoying our hill country scenery. The wounded nephew said, "Huh, that's nothing. I've been riding fences and looking at the scenery upside down."

After much dickering about prices, since others wanted Uncle Carl's farm too, we have bought it. I think it has always been our unspoken dream. Since he was in ill health for some time and unable to work there will be much to do, especially on the barn and all the fences.

We will take our cattle and machinery up there and just enough old furniture to live in the house through the summer, then migrate back to the valley in the fall. I think it will be fun and the adventure will outweigh any hardships.

Ever notice when you mow the grass toward the end of the week that for the weekend you have a lovely green lawn inside too?

Labor and Management

I don't know how a husband and wife business in the city works—what division of administration is made—but out here on the farm there is no question about that. As I trot back and forth the length of the barn fetching milker buckets, carrying out pails of milk, changing milker straps and washing cows, I know I ain't management.

Some weeks a writer's brainwork yields about as much profit as a one-row strawberry patch in robin country.

Up On The Hilltop We Go

Moving the cattle up to the Stump Ridge farm turned out to be almost more adventure than I could stand. Between the pasture gate in the valley and the barnyard on the hill there are five side roads, Star Valley, Towerville and a few strange barnyards to entice them from their journey.

We had a lot of help but that wasn't enough to let me just relax and follow. I ran, I screamed, "Head 'em off from Jones Hollow, Don't let 'em turn into Wee's drive." I was a scatterbrained Leghorn pullet flapping my wings and squawking but we got them there. And I collapsed.

Seminars, classes and courses are popping up everywhere teaching "how to grow old." I seem to just keep on doing it without any help.

Horse Language

Terminology from horse and buggy days stays with us even though that means of conveyance is long gone. I'm often told to hold my horses or that I'm not pulling my weight. Sometimes I hear, "She's got the bit in her teeth," or that I have kicked over the traces. Looking for a lost shoe I was told to gee a little and I would put my hand right on it.

So I wasn't surprised the other day to hear a grandmother say, while complaining about the brakes on their car not being too good, "I want to drive something that will stop when I yell 'Whoa!'"

Viva La Difference

Farming in the valley didn't prepare me for life on the hill. I didn't expect to be this wet. In the valley I did. Sitting out in the cow pen up on the meadow I never got this wet. Wading across the creek, barefoot or in canvas shoes, I never got this wet.

A southwester, slicker and boots should have kept me dry. But rain poured off the hat, down the coat and into the tops of my boots. They were protection only from poison ivy or snakebite and I have killed the poison ivy with 24D and there are no rattlesnakes on Stump Ridge.

Rain was coming down in sheets when I splashed through the barnyard behind the cows and as I walked in the barn door Station WISV was playing Just A-walkin' In The Rain, which I didn't appreciate much.

There are other ways this ridge living surprises me. In the valley I always enjoyed faintly hearing frogs singing way down alongside the creek in other people's swamps. I tried with the help of several enthusiastic nephews to transplant some frogs to our own swamp for closer listening. The boys caught the frogs and brought them but the whole bunch must have migrated back.

So when we moved up here for the summer I thought frog-listening days were over and we would have to drive down the hill to hear them. Instead their singing in the puddles around the barn and tobacco shed is deafening.

And in all the years of our cows wading rocky creek bottoms or walking the gravel road to the meadow they never got a rock wedged between their toes. Toes? Toenails? We found that a lame cow had a rock embedded there and festering.

In the valley killdeer were everywhere. We found their nests among the rocks beside the creek. We found them only because one of the parents did the "bird with a broken wing" trick to try to lure us away. I thought they were a valley bird but here they are wheeling and crying over the highest cornfield. I won't try to find their nests between the rows but I hope their babies, which hatch fully feathered and running, are out of there before harvest.

The difference between a good farmer and a poor farmer: the good farmer expects to take care of his land and livestock so that they will take care of him; the poor farmer expects his land and livestock to take care of him. Period.

36

Sunrise-Sunset

A ridge-dweller for only a few months, already I am reluctant to drop down into the valley to go to work at the Gays Mills Independent. There's hardly a morning that the sun doesn't come up like a ball of fire through the horizon haze and when I get the cows at five I know just what kind of day it will be. At home in the valley we never saw a sunrise—not a real one—nor a sunset.

From up here we can see the Kickapoo River valley and it looks like an elongated bowl of whipped cream. Sure enough, I drop down Stump Ridge hill, drive down Tainter and Johnstown Valleys, turn the corner above the Kickapoo bridge and there it is—whipped cream.

Back home after quitting time I can go after the cows again, this time watching the sunset pull a rosy curtain across the day.

And Away We Go

Exactly one-half year from the time we moved up on the hill we came back down to the valley. Much faster. Stump Ridge has a long, steep road and the cattle started fresh. They stampeded once and the long-legged nephew ran said legs off through a pasture to get around them.

Just crazy they acted, the whole way until we got them to the meadow, their familiar summer territory still almost a mile from home. There they settled down and continued the trip their old gentle selves. Feels good, this two ways of life and there are few dull moments.

One of the biggest mysteries to a farmer—how much hungrier his cows are when he has to buy hay.

Not Guilty

The way it was, Judge, I told him there was this funny noise under the hood when I started out driving and after a while it goes away and then when it doesn't once in a while after every third or maybe it's the fourth clicking noise there's this whoof like the thingamajig that was clicking got tired and puffed a little and usually after while it quits but don't you think I ought to know what makes it do that? And he just said, "Hmmm."

Then I said when the heater isn't blowing loud and I can hear good there's the darndest tapping alongside the car or I think it's alongside the car and it sort of sounds like somebody was throwing something at me and it's hitting the car but I never see anybody and if it should be a wheel getting ready to fall off we sure ought to do something about it before it does don't you think? And he just said, "Hmmm."

Then I told him going down the hill once something went boom, not a big boom but definitely a boom and if the car is going to blow up don't you think we ought to take it to somebody and find out? And when the road is bumpy there is a sort of ping-ping around my feet and if I put on the brake something goes squeak and sometimes it's more like squirk and when I turn the wheel there's sort of a jingle only it sounds like gurk-gurk and then sometimes there is an all over buzzing or whizzing and shouldn't we do something? When I looked at him he was asleep and that's when I hit him, Judge.

Acquitted? You mean no jail sentence? No fine? You are so kind and understanding, Your Honor, thank you, thank you, Madam Judge.

———

I heard a man talking about his wife's ambitious nature. He said, "She goes at cleaning house like she's killing snakes."

———

Back at our sunrise at 10, sunset at 3 home in the narrow valley I vow that we won't do this uphill/downhill living many years; that we will build winter-proof housing for the cows and for us—in that order—sometime soon. As I approach the twilight years, as they say in retirement brochures, I hope to see every beautiful dawn and twilight that hilltop living offers.

Summer was fun but full of frustrations. Get ready to bake a cake—where's the flour? In the valley. Need some bleach for the laundry? It was forgotten at the other place. Wash my hair and where are the rollers to set it? You know where. Sudden company? Extra sheets? Yeah.

And it was getting cold up there. We hadn't bothered to put up a heating stove in the kitchen so I sat holding my coffee warming my feet on the fender of the Round Oak. Shut my eyes and soaked up the warmth. Smelled an odd odor. Opened one eye and saw smoke curling up from my shoe soles. Life may not be perfect but it is verrry interesting.

———

Foster Mother

Little Joe is a tired old tomcat now. He is shirking his longtime job of caring for any batch of motherless kittens we happen to have here on the farm. But he has a successor, an ornery but diligent one.

Spike, what you might call right in the prime of his young cathood, takes time from his tomcatting around the country and every

38

day comes to the barn carrying a mouse for the kittens. And he doesn't even like the kittens. Most of the time he is mad at them. Hot dog, is he mad.

But up through the pasture he comes, calling that plaintive, coaxing cry you expect to hear from a devoted mother cat. He brings the fat mouse up to the barn, sits down and waits. Whichever kitten gets there first makes a greedy swipe at the mouse and hooks it. Spike always lets go but when his mouth is empty he snarls, spits and like as not slaps that kitten head over mouse dinner. A rotten personality inside a good provider.

Boys grow so fast that last year's short, pudgy kids are this year's six-footers. And when a couple of six-foot tag teams start wrestling the furniture and windows can suffer. One nephew who wore short Chubbies last summer is now so tall and thin that he looks like the last half-mile of galloping consumption.

Kidspeak

I'm readin' to Grandma. That's such a nice thing to do for old ladies.

Sh, everybody. I just got Grandpa to sleep.

You can't spank me, Mama, 'cause I'm sittin' on it.

I know you said it was in the right hand drawer. Well I used my right hand to open it didn't I?

Hey, Mommie, come look at the floodpuddles.

A young mother of a toddler called, "Where are you and what are you doing?" A faint voice came back, "Nothing you will have to spank me for."

I know it's raining, Mommie, 'cause the puddles are blinking.

Weather Forecasters?

Woolybear caterpillar watchers are claiming a hard winter is coming because most of their coats are black. Shucks, of all those I have seen when biking or riding, there are just as many whose coats are more brown than black. Yesterday I found one all brown. I don't care how the rest of you figure the winter weather coming, I'm taking mine from the brown.

Stewards of the Land

Walking down the hall in a nursing home last week I heard an old lady in a wheelchair visiting with her daughter and I caught the word "terrible." I paused to eavesdrop and heard the younger woman saying that some people from the city had bought a neighboring farm. The elder said, "It's terrible the way outsiders are buying our farms. I wonder what will become of it."

As I walked on down the hall I carried on a conversation in my mind as I often do. "Old girl," I said, "I bet your parents or grandparents were once outsiders." And then she would tell me, as old people love to do, how they came here from the Old Country. How they bought land, grubbed out a few acres and planted crops.

Through her story of love, marriage, births, deaths, the various season's work, would run the thread—everyone took care of the land. Then I said, (in my mind conversation) "If you must mourn, do so because we are selling it. Unlike the chicken and the egg question, here there is no question which comes first—we sell.

"Much as I dislike the picture I can see myself or anyone having to sell the farm for money to live on. And don't worry," I said, "about what will happen to the land. I have met many newcomers and almost all are just as concerned about the beauty and continuing worth of the land as we are. That is good stewardship."

Twelve miles—that's how far we walked each time we mowed both Swiggum lawns this summer. I borrowed a pedometer to find out and even though I admit that is one darned long weekly stroll, we can't let the valley lawn grow up in weeds.

Planting tobacco—Dorothy and Pearl, with Punk, Cap and Molly

Seeing Snakes

My oddest pets started with one and have multiplied to three. I knew there was a small garter snake in the garden and to help a small grandchild, who is a screamer at the sight of a snake, I took her to see it each time she came to visit.

It was under a length of black plastic I had spread in the garden to kill a patch of quackgrass. It was. Then one day a second snake had joined the first. This seemed to please our granddaughter. If a snake has a friend it can't be all bad. Then there were three. Now every time any of the seven grandchildren come the first thing they want to do is "go see Grandma's snakes."

I had read that mixing honey with water for the hummingbirds would result in that liquid fermenting so I have returned to using sugar and water. This is turning into quite a summer what with intoxicated hummingbirds and pet snakes. Just goes to show life isn't so dull if you look for something exciting. And sometimes even if you don't.

Judging by the response I get to early morning phone calls into town there's a serious agri-urban incredulity gap. Farmers can't believe that everybody doesn't get up at five and town people can't believe that anybody is stupid enough to.

Darn Progress, Anyway

Oh dear, dial telephones are here and I'm afraid it's permanent. No more turning the crank: a long, two shorts and a long, or if I want someone on another circuit one long to get central and say, "Will you get me..." and central saying, "They aren't home. I just saw them walk down the street."

And the unusual sound I have to listen to. Call the Independent office:

735-4413 and this is what I hear. Seven is a snerkplinkclick, three is tickclick, then plinksnerk, snerkplunk, snerkplunk, whirk and tickclick. Please come back, centrals, I'll never get used to this.

Two Lonesome Bachelors

We aren't the only ones wanting us back on Stump Ridge permanently. Pete and Odin, our old Norwegian bachelors, surely hated to see us go back to the valley for the winter.

Every day, beginning with the first one when we arrived, Pete

Eide was there. Maybe twice a day or more. Usually he came walking over barefooted and if I was working outdoors, hunkering down in the shade to watch me. Like when I was building the fireplace he hunkered down and kept saying, "You'll never do it." Accent on the never.

Then every evening Odin Larson drove his old car over and then Pete rode. Odin was 80, I think. Pete? Maybe a little older than me, anyway we learned to waltz and schottische from him. Sometimes we played cards. Or just sat and gabbed. I loved to hear Odin's broken Norwegian. He had come to America as a young man and taught himself to read English.

He had lived well above the Arctic Circle and scorned lutefisk. "We didn't have to treat it with that junk," he said, and was less than enthusiastic when we had them over for a lutefisk supper.

When the scientific son-in-law and his family bought a small trailer house and we set it up out near the pines they came as soon as school was out and stayed until just before Labor Day. Then it was one happy summer for Pete. He loved to play croquet and the game was only taken down for mowing. The SSIL was his idol and he dearly loved to hop on the back of his motorcycle and ride back between the fields and down the lane. Even enjoyed the time his dog caused them to wipe out. I often think of how much joy we brought to them and they returned.

⎯⎯⎯

Do you play around with Tom Swifties? Here are two of mine: I just swallowed a needle, she said pointedly. Your Axminster tripped me, he said ruggedly.

⎯⎯⎯

Best of The Four Seasons

The Lord is generous to us here in the four-seasons country. He gives us autumn, a boon of beauty and respite for the summer-weary; epilogue to the urgent season; prologue to sleep; an interlude for taking stock and counting blessings.

No days are these for looking back too far, time seen in life's rear view mirror is gone much too fast. This is the season of now. Each day is a jewel to be treasured in the eyes and the senses against the time this high blue dome has become slate gray and low.

Colors are rich now, as if the artist had no time for thinning, and odors are rich, too. Wild grapes and elderberries weight down their branches along dusty country roads; apples blush crimson and their numbers and weight bend tree branches almost to the ground.

In tobacco growing country green plants hanging in the curing sheds are slowly turning fragrant chestnut and autumn with a lavish hand flings flowers of a brighter, deeper hue than spring's pastels. Golden pumpkins dot shock-tufted cornfields.

Poets speak of springtime, of balmy breezes and faint perfumes, of dancing lightly around a Maypole while linnets warble a gentle song, of hummingbirds bussing delphinium blooms and the languid warmth of a springtime sun. And of being young.

I want to run through forests' crackling brilliance, my nose stinging from the frosty air; catch the walnuts and the hickory nuts as they patter down among the fallen leaves; bump a vagrant bee trying for one last load of nectar and so weary from the summer's work he can't fight back; clutch a balloon spider's gossamer swing; help every woolybear caterpillar safely across the road and do the same for every frog in low country; dip a spoon in a bubbling sorghum pan; listen to the bluejays try to outshout their cussin' cousins, the crows; and gaze long at the harvest moon.

I want to dig potatoes, split and haul in fireplace wood and kindling, heap high some golden straw over fragile flowers, bring in some of autumn's splendor. If ever I should wish to trade my decades for a scanty score of years, if ever I should wish to be young again it would be in fall.

―⚬―

Shorts

The cats run regular triplines back and forth across our barn as we do chores. And I can see from my position on the floor, elbow in gutter, foot in pail, nine reasons why, if we continue to farm, we should install some kind of automatic milk conveyor system.

―⚬―

If all the exercise wheels in the country were rolled end to end we could measure bursitis by the mile.

―⚬―

When I go to the barn in something different, for instance green slacks instead of my usual blue jeans, the cows ignore the hay I am forking up for them and study me from way down the feed alley and way past, stretching out their heads to smell my different slacks or shirt and even getting a mouthful to see what it tastes like. Just goes to show all females are clothes conscious—even those who don't wear any.

―⚬―

43

Tornado!

The big dog lay by the doorstep, in his eyes a sadness not seen in human eyes—deep, worried, uncomprehending. And I, there to get pictures and a story for my section of the Wisconsin REC News, felt like an intruder.

The smell of death rose and fell as the breeze came and went and when the breeze grew stronger the big dog raised his head uneasily, lifted it higher, looked out across the hills, then down the road I had just come. Sighing, he dropped his head on outstretched paws, closed his eyes, breathed hard, then closed his eyes in uneasy, twitching sleep.

Chaff beside the barn foundation pushed up, so small a movement only one watching that spot would see. Straw specks slid down and in the middle of the tiny heap appeared a nose, then two shiny eyes, then a mouse. It, too, looked at the still world but with furtive urgency, then scurried this way and that, looking for food.

Sounds of a car approaching came down the dusty road and the dog ran toward nearby woods. The mouse sat up on its haunches then scuttled under the mound of chaff.

Sun sparkled from the auto's chrome as it swung into the yard. Sun glanced off eyeglasses worn by some of the people getting out of the car exclaiming, "How terrible, to lose everything you own in just a few minutes" and "What a frightful storm that must have been" "How sad" and "What a pity."

Then "Hey, look what I found. A toy truck. Darn, there's one wheel missing or I could take it home for my grandson." And "Here's an undershirt that might fit one of the kids, might as well take it, these people will never miss it" and "Hey, there's a dog. Here mutt—well alright, you unfriendly brute."

As more shiny cars drove into the driveway to park everywhere people scrambled out and around the farmyard, voices called back and forth, toes poked at debris, cameras clicked. The dog went into the dark shadows of the woods. Looking back over his shoulder, he went. Daylight faded and people left, complaining that they could no longer see to find anything they might like to take. The big dog came back out of the woods, carefully picking his way through rubble and around shredded bushes and trees. The chaff pile moved, lifted, and the hungry mouse braved the open to scamper around the tumbled stone foundation and into the cluttered cavern where the barn had stood.

Padding slowly through the farmyard, the big dog reached the doorstep and stretched out there, the uncomprehending sadness still in his eyes. And in the quietness of approaching night he lay there, guarding the home that was gone. Waiting for the people, his people, the center of his universe and his whole life, to return.

Waste Goes To Waist

I sure wish he didn't hate pigs. Garbage can complex causes a housewife a lot of trouble as she tries to get her shape back into shape for the bathing suit season. Feelings of guilt at having to throw away "good food" are the problem that could be solved if every household kept a pig that really needed all those leftover spoonfuls of mashed potatoes, whipped cream, creamed carrots. It's what we hate to see go to waste that goes to waist.

Walk In My Shoes

We waited for the final heifer, Ella, to have her calf last week. We waited through three cold rains, gale winds and a snow flurry. Not even such weather convinced her she should trust more than her head through the barn door.

Our strategy with barn shy heifers has been to let them have their calves wherever they choose, then by hook or crook, gunny sack sling or just bare-handed grip we would get the calf into the barn and the mother would follow, indignant, yes, but she would follow.

Winter or an unreasonable facsimile caught us still waiting for Ella. On Thursday she looked so

Marjie in dress that won her trip to State Fair

miserable—overdue, too—that we tried to drive her into the warmth and shelter of the barn. Every time we got her partly in the door, stumbling over the frozen surface of the cow pen or breaking through thin ice to get her there, she wheeled and headed for wide open spaces.

A neighbor came along, was welcomed warmly, then we got her back to the door, linked hands behind her and practically lifted her through the door and herded her into a pen. Now we are treating her large, caked bag and keeping an around the clock watch over her.

I understand there are city people who envy us farmers our independent, outdoor lives and would like to try it themselves. I think before they take any final step they should meet Ella.

The Boss was counting up the number of SMV (slow moving emblems) he will need for tractors, trailers, machinery. Wonder why he was looking at me so thoughtfully.

Down Hill—Up Hill

That Mother's Day was nothing to brag about but then neither are some of us mothers so I guess the day was typical of the species. But why our first weekend back up on Stump Ridge had to be so beastly cold and windy must be one of those secrets between Fate and Mother Nature.

Summer home—a polite name for a building that is too cold to live in during winter. And comes this weather, politeness blows out the window, the door, the cracks in the paperboard walls. But this moving twice a year helps with housecleaning. It's easy to clean cupboards and drawers when they are empty. More importantly, you learn to live closer to the bone and throwing away.

Again, moving the cows was the biggest job. True to his word, the Boss let me be the receptionist at the top of the hill. But he didn't lack for help. Every nephew, niece and all families along the way kept the cows on the straight and narrow. That is not an easy job since they have become seasoned travelers and like to go on exploring side trips.

Every year about the middle of June I give out un-asked-for advice to newlyweds. This year I can't seem to get in the mood. Last year I said go ahead and get married—two can live as cheaply as one if both have jobs. If it was so then with the economy now stumbling more at every step, how can I give any advice but—don't? What am I saying? We got married in the Great Depression when hardly anybody had a job.

Summer Hurries By

Second crop haying has run into first; second crop robins are following overworked mothers, begging to have food shoved down their throats that they could just as well pick up for themselves. Second crop rabbits are joining the first crop, now adolescents, along the road out the ridge—each one undecided about the safety of the side of the road it is on, compared to the other side and predictably changing.

Asparagus has gone ferny, blackcaps dried up, no-see-ums replaced by bigger, not always harder biting see-ums. Clannish swallows and offspring by the dozens line the electric wires between house and barn like black beads on a string; bumblebees have their homes well established in the old hay. I heard my first cricket. Don't the summers go fast?

Remember that old "who was that lady" joke? I have a new version. Taking care of grandchildren last week while their mother had mumps I thought to get a little sympathetic cooperation from the three-year-old so I said, "Please pick up the toys, Honey, it's hard for me cause I'm an old lady." She said, "You no lady, you Grandma."

Personality Plus

Non-farmers would find it hard to believe that there are as many different personalities in a dairy herd as there are in a chorus line. And to the directors of each group this fact is probably equally interesting as well as exasperating.

For instance in every herd there are slowpokes and nervous Nellies, placid plodders and quick kickers, affectionate and vindictive. And it's one of the ironies of fate that the cow that combines the best of all traits is the one who will swallow hardware, break a leg or develop incurable mastitis.

Greedy would be a good second name for our young Molly. She stretches, cranes her neck, stumbles and flounders in her stanchion until she has licked up every last speck of her own grain and all of her neighbor's that she can reach. And then again, Rosita ignores others' food. No plate-scraper, her. And should you hear a cow crying about her troubles or moaning and groaning about having to get up and head for the barn, that will be Cindy the complainer.

Does a young heifer follow too closely and crowd you to be petted and scratched, that's Isabel. Does one shy away at your touch? That's Katy. Are a pair of brown eyes watching you over a brown shoulder, that's inquisitive Fawn. Unconcerned about what is happening, whether Laddie is helping her eat her feed or grandchildren are running up and down the feed alley, that's phlegmatic Big Ruby. Dainty stepper—Ruthie; clumsy stumbler—Dolly; aggressive shover—Sara; timid retreater—June.

All these varieties of personalities make life interesting for a farmer. And sometimes they give reason for conversation about and to the cow at the moment. But probably the toughest type of all, and this

47

is a problem in our herd right now, is the buddy-buddy. Two heifers raised together are now grown and inseparable unless confined in the barn. They like each other, that's alright, but they also like each other's produce. That's a problem.

Jim served with the U.S. Army in Korea

Farmers and other country dwellers should carry catastrophic (because it will be) insurance with double indemnity for a septic tank caving in on a weekend with a houseful of guests.

Here, Piggy

We were almost late for North Crawford's graduation exercises. A little pig was to blame. The Boss was getting the car out, I came out the door and yelled, "There's a pig." He gave me one of his "Now what are you up to?" looks. You see, nobody on the ridge raises pigs that I know of. And this was a little, bitty white one, too young to go adventuring or whatever pigs dream of doing while behind fences.

The boss had to see it to believe it and then he didn't want to. "Get in the car," he said, "we'll be late." A fate worse than death. I said, "He's hungry" and ran to get a pan of milk. I set it down, a white cat came and began drinking. As I tried to coax "my" pig to drink the Boss yelled, "Come on," and the pig ran across the yard and down the road.

We got down to a side road and there it stood, looking at us sadly, I'm sure. I tried to tell the Boss I wouldn't mind missing the program and all the way I made static about the little lost stranger. He said, "Probably worth about $35" and I was horrified at the mercenary attitude. And I vowed that when I got home I would do some calling and get visitation rights.

⚬

Parents could start their youngsters out in the world with a proper sense of values if, as soon as the kids begin earning a little money they, the parents, say, "Could you lend me $5 until the milk check comes?" I did it to son Jim and never did he ask to borrow from me. Figured I wouldn't have any, I guess.

⚬

Darnit, another stop sign has popped up between me and my job at the Independent office in Gays Mills. It's right at the bottom of Stump Ridge hill. A cop might as well come and get me right now because when I reach that corner, if nobody is coming either way I will zip right through.

I don't know it firsthand but I have read that other states favor those signs that give right-of-way to the car which is on the most important highway. When the view is unrestricted for great distances it seems to me a complete stop is silly. I'll bet the trouble here is that our sign makers don't know how to spell "yeild."

⚬

I'm a good sport. I got up extra early on the opening day of deer season to help get chores done before daylight. Went to the barn so early the cows weren't up and tomcats not home yet. Took a fast run around the farmstead before TJ came out so if there were any deer close I could shoo them into hiding. Spilled salt while cooking his breakfast and wished him luck with my fingers crossed and after he was gone I went back to bed and pulled the covers over my head.

⚬

Pointy Brooms

How do you feel about those old maxims? A penny saved is a penny earned. A stitch in time saves nine. Haste makes waste. No use crying over spilled milk.

Given enough time I could poke holes in all of them. This one I will: A new broom sweeps clean. When I was a kid I was always told to turn the broom often as I swept so no point would form, then hang it from one of those wall contraptions for the same reason.

As the twig is bent the tree does not necessarily grow. Now my broom sits in a corner, sagging to one side. A point is forming while it sits doing nothing but take on the shape I like on a broom.

You can have your new brooms, well-shaped, straight bottoms. I say they can't clean cobwebs out of ceiling corners, get under book shelves and desks and into corners like an old, beat-up, pointy witch's trade-in can.

<hr>

Pearl's Law: If a cow weighing 1,200 pounds steps on your foot, and provided she has four legs, there will be 300 pounds of cow on your foot. Like a lot of laws it is not enforceable. She shifts her whole 1,200 pounds onto that one foot and grinds it down on purpose.

<hr>

Wonderful Wisconsin

I guess a country has no honor among its own prophets because weekend visitors from Iowa pointed out beauties of our landscape that we have looked at a lot but never saw.

We showed them a shale pit gouging one of our hillsides and said, "That is our land," in sort of an apologetic tone of voice, "and it runs clear to the top of the hill." Compared to Iowa's flat, totally farmable land, we felt that it needed an apology.

"What fun," they said, "to own a mountain."

Then we drove and their conversation went, "Look, Ma, there's watercress." They gasped over ridgetop views, deep, cool valleys, weeds. When we took them down Rush Creek they really gasped over the scenery and the wilderness feeling. We smirked as though we were somehow responsible and so deserved their praise.

Not ever again will we take these hills of home for granted. If we do I hope we have sense enough to invite strangers from another kind of terrain so that we may look through their eyes and once again see the beauty all around us. What fun to own a mountain.

<hr>

Kidspeak: If I have to count more than five I will have to take off my other mitten.

<hr>

Diary of a Midnight Farmer

Monday night cooling off nicely stretched out in a lawn chair with a tall, frosty glass. Just getting dark. Almost time for bed. Ho hum. Phone rings. Heifers wandering in a road miles from home. Are they yours? They are. Thanks, Herman Helgerson, for calling a halt and making them about face.

Thanks, Andersons, for getting them past your place before we could get up there. Thanks, Neal Wannamaker, and we should tell you your hay is waist high and ankle-tangling and when you cut it watch out for a small ditch just past the middle of the field.

The nephew helping round up and run the heifers home said getting through the field you have to step high but that doesn't help, you fall just as flat. Oh, and Neal, your corn on the other side of the road is looking good. Or I think it is. Kinda hard to tell in the dark. But why did you have to cultivate it just before our heifers went on the lam?

They gentled down and got fairly sheepish before we reached the home gate so the other hazards along the way were ignored. Air was stifling back in the valley and it was too dark to hunt for the break in the fence but we figured that would be no problem. The heifers were just as tired as we were.

Cooling down again with another tall, frosty one. Time for bed. Ho hum. Wonder what that livestock buyer's number is?

—⚹—

Not being much of a housekeeper, I have to stand occasional nasty treatment, such as the Boss writing his name in the dust. But during the World Series I get away with hardly any cleaning at all as long as I keep the television set shining. And don't walk in front of it.

—⚹—

Martial Mouse

Pitching down silage one day I got to thinking about the time years ago that a mouse bit me. And it had a right to.

Back in country school there was only one other girl with me from sixth grade on. There had been others earlier but farmers moved a lot in spring and also some children simply dropped out when they wanted to.

Since I was a farmer wannabe even then, I finagled a lot of overnights with her. And since she liked the freedom of behind the counter in our store, and unlimited amounts of candy, she often slept over with me. I had a problem with my visits to her farm. She always

51

wanted to play with dolls and I thought dolls were silly. I much preferred the barn.

I can't remember if she hated the barn, I don't think she ever said, but it showed. So that fateful visit we compromised. I agreed to play with her dolls all evening if she would spend after school at the barn with me. No, she said, not the barn. But she would play in the silo if I wanted to. An interesting idea. I had never been in a silo.

It was toward the end of winter, most of the silage had been fed out, and we only had to climb two doors to get into the silo. Good thing, me being afraid of height. And what a weird place. We could run around inside it forever and get nowhere. So we did that for a while.

Then one of us saw silage stirring and we froze. A mouse peeked out, saw us, and began running with us after it and, like us, getting nowhere. Then I caught it by the tail.

I stood in the center of the silo, swinging the mouse and screaming, "I've got it." Suddenly that tiny hunk of fur turned on its tormentor. It curved its body up, grasped its tail, climbed it and bit me.

Screaming, this time in pain, I dropped the mouse and stood there holding my finger out, bleeding. We were a couple of serious, worried little girls as we ran to the house to tell my friend's mother what we had done and how I had been bitten. I needn't have worried about our reception. Her mother was a laugher.

She found the whole affair vastly amusing, doctored and bandaged my finger, then soothed my feelings with kringlas and milk. I wrote a theme about it for Language Class and got an A. We chased mice in her silo on a few more overnight visits but I never again caught one. Nor tried to.

Unhappy Hubby

The Boss was quite upset at me a while back and I don't think he had any real call to be. See, one of the grandchildren has been collecting soup can labels for a worthy cause and I only had a couple of open and discarded cans. So I cut the labels off some unopened ones and gave them to him.

Mercy, I heard about it. Seems like when I was gone and he planned on having beans with bacon soup he opened a can and had to eat split pea with ham. Men just don't take to surprises like women do.

Commoners

We are the common people. We start the day dragging, all day we're lagging and by night we are sagging. We have perfectly balanced budgets. Everything that comes in goes out. When we are through working we kick off our shoes and our feet smell—of leather, canvas, sweat, and whatever we were walking in, especially in the case of farmers. And in the morning we never can find our shoes, except farmers, who find them by the smell.

We plant our gardens too thick, spread ourselves too thin. We cry a little—not as much as we could; laugh a lot—more probably than the situation deserves. Our fulfillments never match our hopes but we keep trying. We prefer polkas to opera, chip dip to caviar, a ballgame to polo and our back always itches where we can't reach.

We work too hard, play not enough and now and then have a burst of genius—a sudden wild spontaneous idea which we are apt to let our so-called common sense bury. Our weeks are too long, our weekends too short. We are the common people. There are millions of us. Millions are needed. We are the ones who keep our country going.

Eavesdropping on some teenaged girls talking about clothes I heard: "My slip is still in pretty good shape. I haven't needed any safety pins yet."

Solo Choring

The Boss let me (see the bruises? I'm kidding) do chores alone on opening morning of trout season. I think the truth was that after all my bragging about my ability he was calling my bluff.

Choring alone was worth it—about $10 worth of trout if you had to buy them, or could. No problem after the first half-hour that I lost because the huskiest calves got out—two of them—and I had to wrestle them back into the pen. But I had been smart and started half an hour early so the actual beginning was right on time.

The cows behaved well in spite of the fact that they seemed to miss the boss. Judy, of course, tried to step the milker off. Bessie tried to shimmy it off but the other heifer, bowlegged Sara, usually hard to control, was an angel.

I did find myself talking to them and if anyone had been listening I might have gotten the name of talking to myself and you know what that is a sign of. But I don't believe that because I do talk to myself and anyone who is able to do chores alone certainly isn't. Old, that is.

With the end of the World Series I can once again walk in front of the television set. Had Omar Khayyam lived today and been a TV sports fan his most famous verse might have started like this: A sandwich, a cup of coffee and Thou—absent.

Dorothy with daughter Kristi

—⚏—

Sad Days

To tie up a loose end or two Rosita, the cow with hardware, didn't die. At least not yet. After two visits by Dr. McGlynn her future was sort of left up to her. And for several days I wouldn't have bought her for ten cents for fear I would have had to bury her.

Then one day she wobbled over to the hay we changed frequently to keep it appetizing, took a few halfhearted bites and I thought the magnet Doc had inserted into her stomach was going to do the trick. But she chewed like it hurt, smelled of the ground feed, sniffed at the water, wobbled back and laid down again.

Next morning she didn't come out of the small shelter in the calf pen where we had her sequestered so I went about the chores sure that she had died during the night and I might as well put off viewing the remains until I had to.

Before we were done milking she came out and began eating. Not much at a time but little by little she increased the amount she chewed. Her strength seemed to come back and more importantly, she perked up her ears, a sure sign of her feelings. We must give credit to her magnetic interior. Oh yes, telling someone about her later I was asked what breed she is. When I told him Holstein he assured me that she wouldn't die.

⊂—⧈—⊃ ·

Frivolous Philosophies

Life is two "I'll show them" periods, the first restricted by youth and laws, the second by age and physical limitations. Middle age is sandwiched between them and we are too busy earning a living and raising a family to show anyone anything.

When women take up fishing they become more tolerant of the flexible, hands-extended measurements they once scoffed at. Describing the one that got away, their hands may be even more generously flexible than their mates' but not if said mates are within hearing distance.

Remember that when you get mad at your never-ending tomato crop and say a happy good-bye to the very last one you won't be able to say hello to the first of your own crop until next July.

A thousand crickets outdoors at night make beautiful music to go to sleep by. One solitary offbeat cricket in the bedroom is a jab in the eardrums to stay awake to.

⊂—⧈—⊃ ·

Remodeling Woes

Remodeling and adding to the barn in the valley about seven years ago didn't prepare us for the confusion as we build onto and prepare to upgrade this old barn on Stump Ridge. Getting the cows in and out while it goes on is the biggest problem.

In order to lengthen the barn we had to fence off part of the barnyard which means that all the cows must come in the west door. They have been used to entering on the east side and some crossing to the west side. Some behave and do it correctly but for every five that will there is one that won't and that is enough to throw the whole herd into confusion.

Fanny, Bobby and Rachel amble here and there, poking curious noses into odd corners. Or one of them will stand crosswise in front of about four stanchions. They are so cantankerous that every chore time I find myself ripping out a string of "Good gracious sakes alive" and such.

Practically anyone I talk to brings up the subject of weather and says, "How I dread seeing winter come." Not me. When winter gets here that barn will be done and the cows will be in it. And when I trot out in the morning to do chores I will know they are on the mark, set and ready to be milked.

⁓

Who Did You Say?

A columnist in our daily newspaper claimed that he is unique because he is the only one in the country with a theory about who shot JR. I claim more uniqueness. When I read, in front page headlines, no less, that JR had been shot I said, "Who's JR?" And after it was explained I said, "Why does anybody care?"

⁓

Whirlygig beetles entertained me the last time we went to the Mississippi River. Good thing they did. The fish sure didn't.

⁓

Wrong End Laddie

This rain has made it hard to go get the cows at milking time. They stand around under the trees, reluctant to come out into the rain and head for the barn. It isn't that Laddie is not a cow dog. He goes along with me quite happily and if I can get him to bark just once that starts the herd stirring.

But if he chases a cow, chances are I will have to go back to the woods for her again. You see he goes to their heads and barks up into their faces. Never has learned to go to their heels. Since you have to be smarter than the dog to train one I don't have much hopes.

Everyone has been hoping the rain would quit so we could get on with haying and combining. If it keeps on, have pity on the farmers but especially have pity on their wives. They can't stand much more of the smell of wet barn boots and coats and dogs and the sight and sound of husbands going from one window to another looking for a break in the weather. You see it hasn't even been fit for fishing.

⁓

There is nothing like riding on the back of a motorcycle for accentuating our female figures. I love racing a motorcycle any chance I get but I had never given that a thought. But going down the road in the pickup the other day I pointed out a couple on a cycle ahead of us. The girl passenger was generously proportioned. My husband looked for a while, then said, "That's why we call you broads."

This Old House

Selling the farm in the valley has meant added confusion. We have two housefuls of furnishings, this in the ridge house mostly odds and ends. So we cleaned the garage well and stored the excess until such time as we can build a new home.

Before winter came we did everything we could to make what I call the paper sack shack habitable. The Boss covered every window and door with plastic and one day when snow was blowing across the upstairs rooms I covered those windows with plastic on the insides.

Now we live in a paper sack in a plastic bag. We manage to stay almost comfortable and are grateful to the Jurgensen family for giving us one of the new electric blankets. I guess you could say it isn't your average warm house, though. A glass of water on the night stand froze and in the bathroom the bath mat froze to the floor.

A New Haircut

The Boss resisted long hair, always having the barber give him his usual half-inch GI cut right up until this winter. It's a cold one. Little by little he let his hair grow. But that meant he needed a comb. We had two but he could never find them so complained a lot.

I bought an assortment, about two dozen, just for him. Now after I wash his overalls I find in the bottom of the washer just what I have always found for the last 40 years—nails, washers, staples, nuts and bolts, a little money. And combs.

Here Comes The Barn

The barn now has a roof and work on the inside like installation of stanchions, drinking cups, milker motor, is going along nicely. Before we have it finished it will have that which is more precious than rubies in wine, pearls in shampoo. It will have a barn cleaner. One of the men asked, "You gettin' tired of cleanin' the barn, huh Pearl?"

Truthfully, that is one farm chore I have hardly ever done. Although I do remember one time that if I had a heart condition I would have popped a gasket. Not exertion, just mad.

It was cleaning by hand and I was pushing the shovel quite easily along the bottom of the gutter when a cow stepped backward and down and put her hoof right in the middle of my shovel. And stayed there. That is one thing about cows. They aren't weak-willed. If they take a stand, whether on a shovel or a foot, they hold it.

But that's neither here nor there. What matters is that we are beginning to get smart and realize that while we truly love farm life, push-buttons can make the life more lovable.

And The Cow Comes First

When a hill farmer's well gives out there is no question of priority. When the shallow well in the valley had problems we simply turned the cows out and they went to the creek for a drink. Here everything marks time while whatever is wrong with the water system is righted. We go down to our old spring for drinking and cooking water but we can hardly take the cows or bring them enough.

To hilltop farmers well drillers/pullers and plumbers are the hands down VIPs. I can be anxious to wash clothes, scrub a floor, take a bath—no matter. The cattle need water—that is the only important thing in the day. Unless you are a cow you get no respect.

—※—

What happened to summer? Seems like it was only yesterday that I planted dahlia bulbs that today I must dig up. Only yesterday I dragged out all the lawn furniture that today must be put away. Only yesterday that I was young.

—※—

Midnight Meander

City people have no idea of the problems facing farmers any hour of the 24. If they could hear of some that are not found in the pages of peace and tranquility stories maybe they wouldn't be as anxious as some appear to be to trade what they think is the city rat race for an idyllic dream.

Which leads me into a for-instance I hope to never go through again. An electric fencer that wasn't functioning, discovered after dark, was the introduction. We were keeping an eye on a cow that we suspected might develop milk fever. Along about 10—p.m. that was—I volunteered to be the one going out to take one last good look at her before we turned in "because the cows are so accustomed to me."

They are. But I had forgotten that usually when I walk among them I am taking them to a new pasture. They remembered. Not only that, the whole herd got into a frolicsome mood. Like one said to another, "Whee, we're going to a party." Then they all kicked up their heels and ran after their Pied Piper—me.

They ran me down. The only place I felt safe, even waving a high-powered flashlight and cussing in cow talk was on the other side of the electric fence. It was then I discovered the wire off three insulators. This allowed their only deterrent, one slim wire, to rub three metal posts and hang just a foot off the grass.

Not knowing how much power was coming through I didn't dare put the wire back and in fact with 30 curious, cutting-up cows I didn't even dare linger long. So I hurried past, swinging the flashlight in the faces of the lead cows and then back along the wire to show them there was a jolter, such as it might be, in place there.

The end of the feeding lot came and none too soon for me and I swung the leaders like cowboys do in western stories and as they milled around with the rest following in a tight circle I dropped over a shallow bank and rolled out of their sight. Wiping my brow and heaving a quiet sigh of relief I sneaked around the pines and back to the house.

I reported that our milk fever suspect must have been alright, she certainly had been just as frisky as the rest, and we decided that the wisest course was leave the fence alone and hope their dance had left them as ready to rest as we were.

The old saying goes: "Never criticize a man until you have walked in his shoes." I think farm—city understanding would benefit from the practice. I'm willing to learn about urban problems, metropolitan miseries, sidewalk syndromes, but my city exchange is going to have a hard time adjusting to my shoes. They are covered with mud and such like that.

⸺⁂⸺

It's rained so much this summer that our barnyard is deep and slushy and my feet have quit smelling like feet.

⸺⁂⸺

Laugh, Uncle Carl

The farm has been host to several teenage birthday slumber parties in tents this summer. If you don't know from experience or imagination what they are, the opposite of gloom is a good description. As we lay chuckling at the squeals and giggles coming from the tent not far from our window I hoped that the dour, too hard working bachelor farmer who owned it before us and lived an entire lifetime believing there was no time for fun—I hoped his spirit was listening—and laughing too.

⸺⁂⸺

Life Is So Exciting

Life gets just too exciting on a farm for an old lady with a nervous disposition. All these years I have been surviving, but just barely, the nerve-wracking times while kittens learn that cows' feet are not for playing around, their tails are not for swinging from and their warm stomachs not for going to sleep below.

More fingernail-biting time comes when Laddie has to learn that if he chases a neighbor's pickup simply because it contains a couple of dog passengers he must cope with a pickup wheel; and through the terrifying presence of bumblebees in the barn.

These last may be the death of me yet. Or the cause of screaming meemies. Outdoors my fear isn't so great—they make a lot of noise and after a few awkward swings with the dog's dish, an old frying pan, a cake plate, whatever I can grab, the ugly monster is dispatched.

In the barn it's a bee of a different buzz. I can't hear him because of the noise of the milking machine motor and the chugging of milker units. So it isn't uncommon for me to be hunkered down beside

Grandpa Swiggum and little Mark Briggson

a cow and glance aside to find within inches of my nose a big, silent (because of other noises) bee looking at me in a threatening manner.

For such emergencies we keep an old badminton racket midway in the barn. Without it here he would be milking alone. I'm no great shakes at aiming a bat but with enough wild swings the bee either lands in the gutter or somewhere that I can stomp it or it sails out the door looking for a safer neighborhood. As if bee, collie, cat and cow were not enough, the other day Sam, our resident squirrel, went up the transformer pole out by the driveway. It had to be simple curiosity, not fear of Laddie that sent him up the pole. He knows he can safely run past within a few feet of Laddie's nose and he won't give chase. Maybe it was like people climbing mountains simply because it's there.

I held my breath while he went clear to the top instead of doing the usual squirrel stunt of playing around on the transformer itself, making contact—fried squirrel. Linemen climb a lot of transformer poles because of curious squirrels.

The uncertainty of his future made me so nervous that I put a pile of sunflower seeds (he's a glutton for them) under the pole where they were clearly visible from the top, took Laddie in the house and avoided the windows. Sometime later I forgot myself and glanced out the window. There he was, back in his own oak tree. Life is just too exciting.

Our old bachelor neighbors are learning the modern way of eating out—sitting in a car outside a restaurant. And after a couple of supper trips they made an urgent request—that I change my barn shoes before we head for the drive-in.

More Excitement

Calves at the wrong times and in the wrong places cause us a lot of trouble. Sara picked a hot day out in a pasture bordered by thick brush and a gully to have her calf. We didn't dare leave her and the calf there until she might or might not bring it to the barn so we carried the calf, head and legs flopping in all directions, to the pickup parked nearby.

The Boss loaded us—me and the calf—into the back of the pickup and with its mother following we made the trip. Experience has taught me to never ride sitting downhill from a nervous calf so I arrived at the barn only bumped, bruised and shaken, minor complaints considering the possibilities of such a ride holding down a potential small stampede.

That night I checked another cow and returned to the house in triumph to announce "Anyway, Dummy was smart enough to have her calf right now in the cow pen." When he came back from checking on her he snorted, "She's not so smart, her calf only has three legs." I wonder what kind of life other farmers lead.

Beatitudes For A Flower Gardener

Blessed are they who plant flower beds near roadsides to be seen by thousands of passersby. A joy to the spirit, a balm for the troubled soul.

Blessed is the gardener who, being told at fulsome length of the beauty of a certain flower says, "Wait, I will get a trowel and give you a root start."

Blessed is the gardener who can tell you the name of every one of his blessed flowers, even the most rare.

Blessed is the flower gardener who picks lovely blossoms, preserves them in various ways, then turns them into works of art that will keep forever on a shelf or until given away, whichever comes first.

Kittenish Cow

We have a first here on Stump Ridge. And I hope it's a last. We have a cow that bites. Every year when we bring in the young stock from summer pasture they are put in stanchions, which is a new experience for them but they usually adjust quite well. What is harder for some is to learn to press down the trigger in the water cups so that they can get a drink.

For a time we must check the younger heifers to see that they aren't going thirsty. This means pressing the trigger down by hand and holding it while she drinks. If she has learned by herself she simply ignores what we are doing until she does want a drink, then gets it for herself.

Some need help for a long time. Either they are slow learners or too short in the reach. So we stand there holding the trigger down while water gushes out and she drinks until she has her fill.

Little Susie's next stanchion neighbor is pushy Pam, friendly enough but unable to mind her own business. While I water Susie her nosy neighbor nibbles on my arm, licks it with her sandpaper tongue and almost takes the skin off. Before Susie learns to help herself it looks like I will have another first—a hickey by a cow.

Men!

Men have a deplorable tendency to make fun of women for their alleged subjection to the whims of fashion. Ha. Men. When I cleaned our closet—while he was gone all day fishing of course—I discarded more white short-sleeved shirts, tight-legged pants and skimpy ties than you could shake a steam iron at.

He was somewhat upset and said I should have saved them because "they might come back in style." Ha. There isn't room in the closet for all that stuff, what with my dirndl skirts, cancan petticoats and saddle oxfords.

—⟨≡⟩—

Olden Days

Funny how old sayings keep popping into today's conversations. Take when the days begin to lengthen the cold begins to strengthen." Remembering all the years of trying to get our tobacco stripped before New Years, it happens a lot.

Looking through a catalog I thought of that old saying: "There's nothing new under the sun." That one is true, too. In the ladies' undergarment section I found "Enhance the feminine figure with new molded derriere shapers." Back before my time (I said before) they were called bustles.

—⟨≡⟩—

A petunia expert tells me that flowers on the wane must be picked off or the plant will stop blooming. Being a third-degree black thumb I pay attention to all free advice. Problem is how to tell if a petunia is just coming or just going.

—⟨≡⟩—

From Korea

Son Jim sent a clipping from the Pacific Stars and Stripes: "Louis Biddle of Soldiers Grove took the world cheddar cheese championship away from Ervine Cutt of Ontario." Jim had learned that before we did and he's in Korea.

By the way, before you pack your Christmas gifts to send overseas: Don't send money. Not even a buck tucked between pages of a good western story—like I did. Nor in the pocket of a sport shirt he requested for off-duty wear—like I did. Nor tucked among the antlers of Dasher and Dancer in his Christmas box—like I had planned to.

Seems it's against regulations to have American money in their possession. And it seems like somebody in the military hierarchy could have tipped us off—spread it all over the newspapers—so that we wouldn't leave our men open for disciplinary action.

— ·

Hey, Doc

The grandchildren are in the barn a lot, wide-eyed and open-eared all the time. Playing doctor one day in the house the seven-year-old bustled into the three-year-old's room with her medical kit and asked, "Anybody here sick? Anybody need a shot?"

"Nope," little Jimmy said, "I got milk fever and you gotta kick me to get me up."

— ·

Contrary Cows

As we begin keeping the cows in the barn for longer periods of time we get reacquainted, especially with those who have unusual personalities. Or none, like Brindle who is always so tired she doesn't want to stir and is harder to get up in the morning than the Boss.

Meanie—she is small but not named Meanie for nothing. Just plain ornery all the time. Mabel. She's ornery too and would rather kick than switch. Almost broke my wrist once. Both of them are Guernseys.

And then there is Rachel, better known as Dingdong. She does the one-step from the minute the milker is hung on her strap. If it had a clapper it would be ringing. She is good-natured but a squeezer. Likes to stand in a stanchion with a ceiling support to her right so she can get me against it when I step in beside her, then squeeze.

— ·

Says our mother of three small wall-climbers: "Nothing revives a tired child like putting it to bed."

— ·

What A Life!

Here on Stump Ridge the cows are freshening late this year. Usually they will be having their calves along in February and March We have modernized our barn but never managed to modernize our thinking toward having year-round milking, preferring instead to have a winter's lull from chores.

Funny thing about cows. They don't trust people. And when they are freshening after the pasture season has begun they will go as far away from the barn as they can get to have their calves. It must be instinct because the trait is just as common among first-calf heifers as old cows.

So the other night when we were short one heifer at milking

Wayne and Marjie Jurgensen's first car. Jim Swiggum in driver's seat, Wayne beside him. David Jurgensen, left; Sanford Swiggum, right.

time we drove as far as we could, then split up, TJ taking the NE 1/4 and I going the far side of the northwest hillside. I found her and was sorry it was I who did. The distance was too great to shout for help so I was stuck with the problem alone.

Sally had gone as far as she could get and that was tight against the barbed wire fence into the wood lot. Her new calf was below the fence in the woods. Not far away on one side was a gully about 15 feet deep. The calf couldn't be left alone while I went for help because new calves do a lot of floundering in their quest for mother and food and a fall into a gully could mean death on the rocks below.

Between calf and mother was a four-strand fence with the bottom wire just ten inches from the ground. No chance there to get the calf standing and walk it back. The top strand was shoulder high. No chance there to lift even a little Guernsey over.

So I shoved it to the fence, rubbery legs up around its ears, just about the way its mother bore it. Then I dug stuff—brush, branches, sod, from under the fence in one small area. It gave me just room enough to drag the calf, stretched out on its side, under the bottom wire. Then I dragged a log to block the 10-inch gap because the stupid calf was already up and staggering down the incline to the fence.

I pushed and pulled to get it a good ways from the fence and on the far side of a brush pile. Was scared. A couple of years ago a neighbor was attacked by a heifer who misunderstood his intentions when he went to rescue her calf. He was almost killed. So I was scared. But Sally only lowed gently as I half carried, half dragged her new, wet calf, wrapped in my barn shirt, to safety. She let me, but her head thrust over my shoulder, then under my arm, was a hindrance.

A run through the hay field and a shout brought stronger help and after we got the calf many rods away from the danger spot we walked the electric fence back to the barn to get the pickup and return. TJ took off one rubber boot and used it for a protector while he put the wire back in place where a cow fight had knocked it loose.

Bobolinks flew up from the hay, warning us not to molest their nests, we could hear whippoorwills in the valley below, a deer started up from the edge of the woods, then stayed motionless while we did the same. Even troubles—on a farm—have a way of turning into pleasure.

Plain Philosophies

Love is wearing a barrette if your hair hanging down in your eyes bugs somebody.

Common sense is trying, but if success is elusive, then reading the directions.

Happiness is not needing to read the directions.

Thoughtfulness is putting your shoes back on if your feet smell.

Sweet Smells

The smell of wood is a smell of youngness. It brings back carrying wood in from the pile to keep the wood box filled, the sound of a freshly kindled fire roaring up the chimney, the rattle of the cookstove lids and the long iron griddle being clanged into place on the two main lids and the nagging worry about what if the house caught on fire yet knowing that our father would never allow that to happen.

So when our old heater in the basement smoked the other day and filled the house with a blue, aromatic haze, it did not disturb me. I wallowed in nostalgia. Then I washed the smoke out of my hair. Nostalgia is alright, but not when you carry it around with you.

⚫────

I was plenty peeved the other day when the Boss dug in my flower bed to get some angleworms and go down on the creek fishing. Later I decided a few upended crocuses were unimportant compared to a supper of fish filets. Making people happy sometimes requires comparisons.

⚫────

Smart Cats

There are no stray cats. That's my belief. Well-meaning people often trot out the theory that stray cats, which they think may have been dumped, are desolate, lonesome, starving creatures. I say that out in the country if you see a cat along a road, that cat isn't lost. It does have a home somewhere. And the home they claim at milking time is whatever home they want.

Over the years our farm cat clan has been swelled by so many cats who came to dinner and never left that I advise the tenderhearted to waste no worry on "dumped" cats. They never stay dumped unless they prefer the wild, outdoor life. And feeding them well and telling them to leave birds alone is useless. You can't tell a cat anything. Certainly not "Begone."

⚫────

Reverse Psychology

The old saying goes, "You can lead a horse to water but you can't make him drink." As spring busts out all over with all kinds of new babies appearing on the farm I realize all over again that horses are much more obliging than calves, which you can't lead anywhere.

The only way you can handle a calf is to make its contrariness work for you. After trying with might and main to pull a calf the length of the barn to his pen, only to have him sit down and dig his feet in, I turned him around, pretended to pull and he sat his way backward to the other end of the barn and into his pen. You do have to be a little bit smarter than they are.

⚫────

Cow Curiosity

Curiosity is not a cat's monopoly. Cows have it too.

I trundled the wheelbarrow out to the night pasture to get some Aida dirt (named for a sister who is always exclaiming, "How I wish I had some of this good dirt down in Madison for my flower beds) and one by one the herd's top brass fell in behind me.

When I reached the best spot—a mixture of top soil, pulverized, decaying green choppings and some other stuff—I stopped and began shoveling. The boss cows, about half the herd, gathered close around me, following each trip of the shovel down to the ground, then up to the wheelbarrow with avid interest.

I deliberately kept those closest interested with sprightly conversation and actions because back at the chopped hay wagon I could see the heifers and insecure cows had taken advantage of my diversion and had stepped up to take the boss cows' places and were eating fast.

It wasn't until the rulers of the herd had escorted me and my load of dirt all the way back to the gate, reaching to smell of the dirt and probably wondering at the foibles of other females, that they realized they had lost control and went galloping back to the wagon.

Confucious say farmer who do night herding should not raise Black Angus.

Men!

Don't let any farmer or farm writer give you that jazz about radio music in the barn making for more contented, happier and productive cows. The volume of our music could not contribute to any female's peace and contentment. It sure doesn't to mine.

But the barn is his domain, his word is law (I think it was in the fine print on our marriage certificate) and the radio is shaking the rafters for one reason only, I'm sure—to drown out the sound of his wife's nagging voice. I complain about this constantly. But he doesn't hear me.

Somebody—a man of course—told me I must stop picking on my husband in my column. So I asked if it bothered him and should I quit. "No, no," he said, "don't stop." So there.

Decisions—Decisions

Everybody should build a house. Probably only one because I'm beginning to suspect that only the hardy can survive even one. Maybe not all women have my traits and troubles. I hate decisions.

And one day last week I was faced with what seemed like a hundred all at once, from every branch of the building industry. The Boss is no help at all. He just says, "Ask her."

Probably when it is done I will wonder how did that happen to be there—I don't remember deciding that. Because most of the questions I answered with "Whatever you think best."

But when all is quiet at the end of the day, carpenters, plumbers, electricians, all gone home and I stroll through the house, going through what will be doors, not between wall studs because that wouldn't be Cricket, I dream:

Here am I in the kitchen (where else?) washing dishes and looking out the window. Here I am in the mud room washing up after coming from the barn and looking out the window. Here I am in the basement, lovely, lovely basement. We have never had anything but a small hole in the ground with a dirt floor—come to think of it, three times that is what we had.

Here by the dining room table—three saw horses and two planks—I can look out the window toward Pine Knob and here by the fireplace (happy me) I am looking out the window at the paper birch, beyond them through the spruce windbreak at a rosy sunset. Yes, everybody should build at least one house. It is like a dream coming true.

Turn Off The Bubble Machine

You have seen those public service announcements or warnings to never take medicine in the dark? Well, I always thought no sensible person would do such a thing unless she knew exactly what she was getting hold of. And I thought I did. See, I had this cold and the cough that followed just hung on.

One midnight I was so worn out and disgusted with coughing that I dashed into the bathroom and grabbed for my own personal bottle of cough medicine, uncorked it, tipped it up and dumped a dollop down my throat. For a few horrified seconds I stopped swallowing, then bent over the sink, spit, choked, gagged and bubbled.

Sick? I thought I would die. It wasn't the taste, which was not half bad. It was all those bubbles. Now I know I will never again take medicine in the dark. And it is going to be a long time before I will be able to watch Lawrence Welk again.

Men!

Didn't your heart just bleed for the Duke of Windsor last week? Neither did mine. There was that story about him making up with the royal family, then the speculation that he regretted having given up the throne for marriage and was considering his life had been a waste.

Maybe I'm a square but it seems to me there is no end to the kinds of worthwhile careers and that first a man ought to amount to something as a man or he will never be any great shakes as a king.

Life With Seven Extras

Last week started like all weeks, with a Monday. But before it was a few hours old it changed. First came Mark Olaf, born as every good farm baby should be, after his parents did morning chores.

Then came Kristi, 6, to be Grandma's go-fer and watcher of Jimmie, 3. In response to almost every call he answered, "I'm in the

Grandpa with Kristi Briggson and Laurie Jurgensen

chicken house playing with the kittens." That place was full of cats because there wasn't much more profit in chickens.

Then, because their parents went to Oak Ridge, Tenn. to make
sure of an apartment for their science scholarship summer, came Laura,
4, pensive and quiet unless struck with a giggling streak—the plum in
her little cousin Jimmie's pudding—and then came Mary, who should
have been.

For Laura has reached the "Get out, we don't want you—you're
a boy" age and as he stood outside the girls' room kicking and screaming, more than likely with a bumped nose from the slammed door, it
was Mary who ran down the hall, put her arms around the tiger in a
tantrum, kissed him on the cheek, then if that didn't sooth him, mur-
mured, "Shall I scratch your back?" Funny how young they learn the
soothing power of a good back scratching.

And then came Barbara.

Now to all grandparents having to prove their child-caring abilities with six: if possible never mix creepers and racers—those who need
rocking and those who need running down. Not unless the package
deal includes a grandma helper like niece Bonnie, in her early teens.

A paragon of patience—what more can I say except that it was to
Bonnie's worn sneakers that Barb crept when she wanted rocking; it was
Bonnie who could tub the older while I washed the little one in the
kitchen sink; she who could scrub dirty faces and not get a whimper and
the supreme compliment: when Jimmie was back home and his mother
asked what he did he said, "Played with Bonnie. She's great." They've
been gone now for three weeks and no matter how I clean and sweep,
even under furniture, I find only one each of many pairs of socks. I
think there is a monster that eats socks, paper clips, bobby pins and
pencils. And another that lays hangers. Or why do they multiply so?

Hay Fights

We have had our annual hay fight and maybe the rest of the
summer can go along smoothly. We both admit that at haying I'm not
much better than nothing and sometimes I'm worse. But come some
evening with 200 bales out and it looks like rain—he is scraping the
bottom of the barrel.

We get out on the side hilly field and yells speed it up a little and
I yell I'm scared and wonder why I like hill country so well but just then
good neighbor Pete comes through the fence and gets roped into helping and he yells take your foot off the clutch and I yell it is off and

hold my foot up to prove it which is a mistake because tractor wheels aren't like car wheels and they turn too quick.

Back at the barn I try to redeem myself by going up in the haymow and throwing bales out from under the elevator until I'm told that I'm in the way so then I go and pet the six cats and 13 kittens. I'm good at that.

Cows are creatures of habit and may react to the unexpected. I'm afraid if I go into the barn wearing a dress they might just jump right out of their bags.

By now you know weird cats and cows make our farm life so happily interesting we could never trade the barn one-step for a sidewalk shuffle short of a problem like senility. But for a while now we haven't had any new tricks among the animals. And then old Charlie took to steaming his whiskers.

The big fat yellow tomcat that I once hauled back to his own home on a neighboring farm, and then he beat me back to the barn, follows us the length of the center alley as we milk the cows.

I carry along two pails of hot water, one for washing udders, the other for dipping inflations. Wherever I set the pails down there is Charlie crowding against the pail, holding his head out over the rising steam. He looks like a man in a barber chair having his whiskers steamed for shaving. He also looks silly.

One Is Enough

Farms are getting bigger. We don't need economists to tell us that. We see it all around us. Individual farmers buy up neighboring 40 or 80 acres or even another whole one to add to theirs. But this time of year we learn all over again that no farm will be big enough for two tomcats.

Hurry Home

Now that Women's Lib, equality and all that are here we farm women have decided that we can only take an academic interest. We know that in the pursuit of liberation, even if we wanted to join a protest march we had better be back in time for chores. Frankly, I like my status quo. I am in charge. He just hasn't noticed.

My husband is about as naive as any of them. He honestly thought buying me a new broom meant that I was going to sweep clean.

Talking To The Animals

Rex Harrison did it and I do, too, but not the same kinds of animals nor the same conversation. Here are some of mine on any day of the week.

To the cats on being rushed as I enter the barn with table scraps: "Stand back, you hungry fiends or I'll get a whip and a chair. Ever hear of mice? Those are the furry little critters in the granary and corncrib. Go hunt."

To the cows as their heads block hay bales I'm feeding: "Get your big ugly heads off these bales or I will rap you on the polls. When you shuttle the hay up and down the alley, as you always do, you will have a second chance to find the best."

To the birds as I take in the washing: "Can't you find a new flyway? Surely you don't need to soar over this part of the lawn? And please, not on the boy's car."

To the kittens who think I fork up loose hay to the cows just so they can play in it: "Out of my way, you suicidal maniacs. Suppose the cows eat you? Suppose I run you through with the pitch fork while you hunt for imaginary mice? You lose one of your nine lives every day."

To a cow as I doctor an injured udder: "Hold still while I put this salve on. Kicking won't get you anywhere but it might me. Stupid, of course it hurts but anybody dumb enough to step on her own teat deserves it."

-⟨⟩-

Statistics—Vital And About Time

During the previous years daughter Dorothy married Otto Briggson, farmer: Kristi, Jimmie and Mark. Marjie married Wayne Jurgensen, science teacher: Laurie, Mary, Barb and Alan. Jim waited a long time to find the perfect one for him, LeAnna, my favorite daughter-in-law. When this clan convenes it becomes as close to a circus as one can get without an admission ticket.

-⟨⟩-

Wrong Twins

I put the cows in early—the Boss was away helping a neighbor—and I noticed that Rosie was missing. We had worried about her, due to freshen any day, so I drove back to overlook the pasture and saw her. With field glasses I could see that she was up in a corner with two calves beside her. Goody. We needed more heifers so I was hopefully happy.

After chores we went back in the moonlight to check her for milk fever, a possibility in a new mother. Cow, that is. We talked

73

quietly to Rosie as we approached, saw that she was chewing her cud, a good sign, then walked home. Her calves lay close beside her and we hoped she would bring them in by morning.

Next morning she wasn't there so we went back to make sure the calves had nursed and were not surprised to discover they hadn't. She is so underslung that only midgets could have found her udders. We wrestled a calf to each side of her, laid the babies down and guided their hungry mouths. Any other cow would have meant getting our heads kicked off. She stood like a tired angel.

Our heifer hopes were thwarted. One was a bull so the heifer was a freemartin. It would have been a struggle herding the three so we again left them there. When I got the cows that night Rosie and the little female were with them.

After chores we drove the pickup back, let down the fence and bumped across the pasture. I ran ahead and got a good hold on the little bull in case he spooked. Then we put him in a gunnysack, loaded him in the back of the truck and I sat (uphill from him) holding and talking to him all the way back to the barn. It was about nine and I wondered what other farmers might be doing.

Hernia—April 1973

I flunked How To Spread Manure On A Windy Day so when husband TJ learned he needed a hernia operation he arranged for a relative living nearby to come daily and clean the barn. But at the suggestion that someone be hired to help me with the other chores—milking, feeding, caring for the calves—my female chauvinism reared its head and I said, "Please, I want to do them myself." Hadn't I been the favorite dependable, unpaid help since day one?

What I really wanted was to be my own boss for a while. So it was with a feeling of elation that I returned home after taking him up to the hospital and went to the barn alone. I stepped in, surveyed both rows of cows and said, "Now you girls are all mine." Chores went well, I got up to see him every day and we talked on the phone in his room. "Hi, Honey, am I getting the hay down OK? Of course I am. No, I'm not being careful throwing bales down the chute so they don't hit the water cup and break it off. I'm carrying them to the end of the mow and throwing them down that hole into the lean-to. Of course I know it's more work. Please, I'm getting the chores done. Trust me.

"Hello, Dear, how are the stitches this evening? Do they hurt? They don't use stitches anymore, they use clamps? And they do hurt. That's too bad. But everything is fine here and you know mean Pam— she doesn't scare me anymore. I stopped treating her like a friend I wanted to make up with and began treating her like an enemy. She hasn't once kicked me on the ankle since I kicked her shins. See, I told you not to worry. You just lie there and recover. I can handle anything that comes up.

"Oh, it's you. Yes, I was busy. You know Lily—she isn't supposed to freshen for a couple of weeks yet. But she is going to now. I just put her in the maternity pen. How did I do it alone? You don't give me credit for good sense, do you. I stacked hay bales across the walks at each end of the barn and chased her back and forth until she gave up and went into the pen. I would appreciate it if you would have a little confidence in me and my ability to cope with anything that happens. We women aren't helpless."

Then one night he called about ten. "What do you mean I sound strange? That noise in the background? That's a cow. Yes, I know it's late to be in the barn but I just thought I should check on Lily—she's alright—and kick up hay and bed again. You know, I always do that and I don't mind waiting. What am I waiting for?

"Well, if you must know, I can't get out. Why? There's a skunk between me and the house. But it ought to go away. Sometime. If it isn't rabid. I am not crying. I sneezed. What is the skunk doing? That's a silly question. What do I care what it's doing? It's out there. That's enough.

"Oh, alright, I'll go peek out and see, if you are so determined to know. It is bumbling all over the garden, nosing through the potato cores and apple peelings I threw out there to plow under and now it is eating something. How do you know from way up there is your hospital bed that it isn't rabid? Now it is going away and I will run to the house." I did, TJ came home but "Do no farm work yet," the doctor said. I was just glad to have the Boss back.

Blizzard—April 1973

It started out to be a two-pie Sunday. With the Boss home from the hospital and weather mild with just a little something hard to identify in the air, it seemed to me the afternoon would bring company and I prepared. A loaf of homemade bread, meat loaf to slice for sandwiches, hickory nut cookies and I made two pies—if I do say it myself as shouldn't, the best banana cream pies of my baking career.

Then I left TJ relaxing on the daybed made up in the living room and went to the barn to lime the floor in case menfolk should drift out there to escape women talk (and check how the wife took care of the barn), lime being the farmer's equivalent of his wife's floor wax.

Along about two some phone calls inquired for TJ's health and

75

said that the callers planned on coming but didn't like the looks of the weather. I didn't either but no still, small voice warned me to prepare. Monday it was too late.

Our problems were no bigger nor worse than mailmen, highway employes, law officers, factory workers—anybody's. Here on Stump Ridge nothing moved on the roads. I'm sure it was the same on flatlands. Nobody could come to help me clean the barn so I had to run the manure out on the ground. No problem. Granted it was no fun to level the pile down to make room under the barn cleaner for the next day's load but it didn't take long, the wind blew so hard snow cut my face and I hurried.

Three drifts, the first parallel to the house, four feet high and maybe 50 feet long; the second drift above the garage doors and extending over to reach the first and the one out by the barn sealing the big doors and reaching into the haymow made me wish I had a coffeepot in the barn and I would have stayed there.

After the wind let up, I think it was Tuesday, Laddie and I found a bare walk following the edge of the drift around back of the house, into and along the windbreak, back to the granary and around the chickenhouse. Eight times on Monday I had to dig out so I could open the milkhouse door. Only seven times on Tuesday.

Inside the barn was another world. I knew TJ was suffering with anxiety but I liked it. Not warm, wind found every crack, but cozy shelter from the storm slashing the windows. Usually extroverts, Laddie and the cats didn't bother me as I did chores. They stayed curled together in the hay at the end of the alley. But three milkings and I had arrived at a real problem. I ran out of milk cans.

I'm not complaining. I was just one of the thousands of farmers having the same problem—cows giving milk and no place to put it. They can't be expected to hold it until a more convenient time.

Imagination and six plastic bags gave me three bushels, a tub and three big boxes of milk. Then there was no place to put it but down the drain. But when things can't seem to get worse they usually get better. Tuesday night son Jim got out from Sun Prairie. The hill was still deep in drifts so nephews Rick and Randy Olson joined Jim in Operation Milk Can.

For almost an hour they backpacked milk cans up the hill on their snowmobiles, their sister Janice and parents, Lila and Orvin Olson, working at the truck at the foot of the hill—tying bindertwine into loops that were slipped over the boys' shoulders. What a sight—the can swinging from the back of the driver.

Only another dairy farmer could understand the relief I felt, knowing that when I milked in the morning I could save that milk as

76

well as transfer milk from unorthodox containers. And nobody could understand TJ's worry and stress while he could do nothing to help, as another dairy farmer could.

In the night the old faithful Utica township snowplow came past and next morning Orvin came early with tractor and scoop to clear for getting the milk out to the road, the spreader in under the cleaner, then Jim went to work straightening out our problems and it was good to ease my burdens onto broader shoulders.

We are so thankful for relatives and friends (and isn't it nice those two categories often come together in the same persons); for a son's boss, Tom Cremer of Expert Construction, who let him off work so he could come help and for the son who would. And for dependable Crawford Electric Cooperative. What if my electricity had failed? And what of my two pies? Tuesday the cats finished them off and good riddance.

⸺⁂⸺

Grandchildren: the Briggsons, Kristi holding Mark, Jimmie in overalls; Barb Jurgensen on Grandma Pearl's lap, Mary and Laurie holding Alan.

It's easy to believe that greens such as nettles, dock, lamb's-quarters are nutritious and will make you healthy and hearty. Did you ever see a puny weed?

Beatitudes for visitors:

Blessed are they who are bright in spirit, never complaining of their troubles and ailments. And laugh a lot.

Blessed are your contemporaries who never look at the underside of your homemade garments. Nor pull loose threads.

Blessed are the ones who tell you they are coming so you have time to pull your seams together, dust the table where the light shines across, comb your hair and hide the ironing.

Blessed are the coffee drinkers who catch you with no cream in the house and insist they really do prefer black.

Blessed are the visitors who, when they insist they really must go, say goodbye and go.

Recuperation

These are strange weeks. Not too strenuous as TJ picked wisely the time for his hernia operation. Nobody could have predicted that blizzard. Milking now is at its lowest. Only one more cow will freshen before he can help. Fay—and I can handle her. To get up and go to the barn alone is the odd part. Not really alone. Laddie always with me and the cats meet us halfway there. We comfort and console each other.

Another Skunk

During Punk's convalescence I encouraged him to go fishing at the Mississippi a lot. One day when he was gone I met a skunk staggering around the house. I did what any sane, as opposed to rabid, person would do. I ran in the house, shut all doors and watched it.

He wandered below a window and I saw an ugly wound in the back of his neck. It kept on all day reeling and falling down and I, owner of a .22 but a poor and squeamish shot, waited. When Punk got home he took the gun, followed carefully (the thing ignored him) to the barn, then shot it. I buried it. An unpleasant incident and one we recall when the wind is from the northwest.

Ideal Idolizers

Grandparents are for considering you the most brilliant, beautiful, lovable people in the world and telling you so.

Grandmothers are for allowing a parade up and down the hall, complete with oatmeal box drums.

Grandfathers are for retreating inside radio earphones then later telling grandmothers, "My, they were certainly quiet this weekend."

Grandfathers are for giving you cards with money in them when other grown-ups seem to think you would only want a package and wouldn't know what to do with money anyway.

Grandmothers are for telling you how your mother, "when she was little, just like you, cut her own hair, just like you, then she took the scissors and..." Mothers are for saying, "Please, Mother..." to grandmothers.

Grandparents are to go visit overnight all by yourself when you just need to get away from it all and are too little to go anywhere else.

⌐#◯ ·

At milking time I shift my voice into falsetto soprano and call "Kitty, kitty." That has been my theory, that it takes a high-pitched coaxing voice to bring the clowder of cats together. Then he shoots holes in my theory, getting the same results by banging on a pail and bellowing, "Come and get it, cats."

⌐#◯ ·

It was colder than a pitchfork handle in a mow facing north the morning I discovered that I hadn't latched the milk house door the night before. And everything was frozen up. It was my fault because I was the last one out. But while he fed in the barn I did a quiet job of thawing water pipes and getting milker buckets ready. No harm done. And husbands don't have to know everything. And they wouldn't if wives didn't have big mouths. Or write a column.

⌐#◯ ·

Bath Time

Old Katy never could read a calendar so it shouldn't have been a surprise when she freshened ahead of time. But it sure was. There is no other way but surprise to describe the sensation of opening the barn door one morning and being greeted by a brand new calf which has traveled the length of the gutter before getting his legs under him.

Down the full gutter he had traveled. And while he appeared strong and healthy—I guess exercise is good no matter where it's done—we couldn't tell the little tyke's complexion. A couple pails of warm, soapy water then a warm rinse and rubdowns with two gunny sacks, an old pile throw rug and a bath towel and he was a handsome black and

79

white. But I wasn't. So that particular pair of jeans, sort of puce color, will go nowhere anymore but to the barn.

Whiskey Baritone

Vaughn Monroe sits at the top of the haymow ladder and complains all the time we do the milking. One of the wildest of this year's crop of kittens, he must have resisted when his mother dispersed the rest. He won't come down so after chores are done I climb the ladder and feed him. Until then he yowls and squawls about his hunger, loneliness, the world in general. And what else can you name a cat that meows through its nose?

City wives: we here on the farm have a few occupational hazards that don't affect you. And when I tell you, you will be glad. See, there is this farmer I know. He came in the house one day and announced, "You'll have to help me find my billfold."

"Where did you lose it?"

"Out in the field when I was spreading manure."

"What color is it?"

"Brown."

Sneaky Me

Now and then during winters when most of the cows were dry and we only milked maybe ten or so I sneaked out in the mornings and let the Boss sleep. Laddie went with me—when doesn't he—but I had to call him back from chasing rabbits around the bird feeders, then call him into the barn or he would wake up the whole north end of the county.

I left the radio and the intruding world silent, swept and fed at a leisurely pace, stopped to scratch an ear here, a tail there. Things went well—my way. I set the milkers aside to feed calves, or curry a friendly cow, carried a bale of hay to the center of the barn so Laddie could snooze comfortably. He doesn't like to be a whole barn length away.

Everything ran like a well-oiled clock. Suddenly the barn door banged open and in stormed the maestro, half angry because he hadn't been wakened and I had sneaked out. He takes over and I become the gofer. But for a little while there I was Queen of the barn.

Reaction

People often ask "How does your husband react to mention of him in your columns?" I have to answer, "Most times I can't tell." But you remember how I said I enjoyed sometimes getting to the barn alone and running the show myself? Well, a few mornings after that he allowed old Queenie to do chores alone and slept in.

Eulogy For A Live Dog

This is a eulogy for a live dog and I tell you immediately so that if you can visualize a happy farm life without dogs in it, then quit reading and go do something else like check your tulip bulbs to see if that warm spell I mentioned fooled them into thinking it was spring. Or shovel a path through the snow which will probably be four feet deep since I mentioned spring or clean the calf pen. It probably needs it.

What brings this on? Our constant companion for 12 years is beginning to look and act like us—old and gray. And get up like us—groaning and complaining. When we walk the farm he follows more than he leads. Where once he teased us to hurry, foraging far ahead then racing back to spring high in the air and bark excitedly, now he lies down and waits if we pause to enjoy the countryside.

Our shadow's shadow mingles with ours as he, too, takes a slower pace. And I think of all the shadows that have followed ours through the years: slim, husky, sleek, furry, tall, short, curling tails and none at all. They had many different characteristics but all had one in common—devotion. None were acquired—like going and buying one. They simply came. And adopted us. And there was never any doubt about their loyalty. We belonged to them. That was all.

Retirement?

The time is coming when we will have to quit farming. I have been pushing back the thought, hoping that before long somebody might invent a way to reverse the clock and the calendar. We haven't even talked about it much, only in elaborately casual ways, like what we might be able to do "when we quit milking cows." Because that, as every dairy farmer knows, is the key that will unlock the ball and chain.

We don't know how much change there will be, or 40 years of habits will allow us. Sadness mingles with my every thought of a new, maybe exciting way of life. How can I say goodbye to the herd when the time comes? How have those before us felt as they watched familiar faces, voices, ways, pushed into a dozen different stock trucks to be hauled away in a dozen different directions?

I will miss the active involved-with-the-cows life. And what will I have to write about when my always unpredictable subjects are gone? On the other hand there will be a plus—a small one. I will never again have to be sad at the sale of a calf or mourn a sick cow if I don't have one.

— ✺ —

Winterizing The Dog House

There are chores that must be done when you admit that winter might finally come. One of those is seeing that Laddie has a warm house when he isn't sharing ours. First I carried a bale of hay from the barn and put against the bottom of the front door. Nobody ever goes to the front door of a farm house.

Laddie thought that was for him, climbed up on it and surveyed his realm. He will be there every sunny day all winter. The bale was so heavy that for the next two I used the wheelbarrow. Those I stacked as a windbreak in front of his house. The southeast wind is the most piercing and coldest.

Then I pulled nails holding two pieces of carpeting as drapes in front of his door, moved them together and nailed them back in place. When we first built his house we thought he might not enter if he had to push through drapes. He did those, now I wondered if a totally closed entrance would deter him.

I added about six inches of fresh straw to that on his floor. It was thin in the middle due to a dog's habit of turning around a lot before lying down. And because I wasn't sure how he would accept a new floor I showed him a juicy bone, tossed it into his house and explained the reason.

He followed me to the garden where I was gleaning the last of the broccoli and a couple of miserable looking cabbages. As I wandered through the garden thinking of what I would plant and where next spring (as gardeners always do) Laddie disappeared. Back at the house I called, got no response, then looked in his house. He was there, calmly chewing on his bone. Approval.

— ✺ —

Shoo Fly

A new kind of fly, that we never have seen before, is plaguing our cows. Face flies. And they are rapidly increasing in numbers. Haven't read where they came from but I sure wish they would go back there.

They have one peculiarity that gives me a chance at trying to eliminate some. They prefer full sun, don't like shade.

So I painted the wall around the barn door with a residual insecticide and as the cows enter the barn all of those flies leave their faces, land on the wall and I can see that some die. But I think I and science are losing the battle. We let the cows out, their faces are quickly dotted with flies. And they, the flies, don't care whose face they sit on.

⊂⊞⊃

Farm Trouble

Water, water everywhere but not a drop in the well. It had rained so much—six inches in one evening—that we had to stop haying and start sweeping water in the basement toward the floor drain. The well went dry off-schedule.

I call it off-schedule because it usually happens when the temperature is well below zero. During a warm, wet spell it took us by surprise.

Only those farmers living on hilltops can appreciate what it means. In every valley there is a creek for the cows and a spring not too far away where drinking and cooking water can be gotten. Oh, we had lots of water. That was the irony of it. But our water was too shallow for the cows to drink and every puddle had a robin or a frog in it.

We discovered the problem after we began the evening milking and since there was nothing we could do we finished chores. Then we went to the valley spring and brought home two milk cans of water for our use. Funny how conserving of water people can become when there is a shortage. I even left the supper dishes although I didn't need an excuse for that.

Then we began calling for a well-puller. The stock tank was almost full but in warm weather that wouldn't last long. Our good old dependable Earl Nelson didn't answer and we kept trying until the telephone operator suggested that their line might be waterlogged. That does happen to buried lines.

We managed to reach a neighbor of his who promised to go see Earl first thing in the morning. Hardly had we finished morning chores when Earl and his well-pulling truck arrived. Our well is so deep, 300-400 feet, that we have trouble often—holes in the pipes, worn sucker rod, other things I don't understand. This time it was bad pipes which had to be replaced. And were.

It worries me. There are not too many men who do this work. And there are thousands of wells. If this ability is not passed on to younger men, when the old retire what a desperate situation we will be in. Come to think of it, some already are. And think of waiting a week or more for water. What is to become of us "all thumbs" people if the community handyman closes his doors and nobody takes his place? I predict the day will come when Jack-of-all-trades makes more money than Joe College.

Farm Trouble #2

My electric typewriter was clattering away, refrigerator and freezer motors hummed, water pipes thumped as cows in the barn drank. Coffee was still hot on the electric stove and the electric clock said 3:25. Then ohm and ampere, watt and volt were as if they had never been.

The silence was like the inside of a cave. Water pressure dropped

Sanford and Laddie

to just that—a drop. The cows had beat me to it. I quit typing—no choice—drank my coffee, wandered around chewing my fingernails and thinking about milking 15 cows by hand. Didn't even think to say I was glad half the cows were dry.

Supper was a pan of sausages and fried potatoes held over the flames in the fireplace, some lefse taken from the freezer and coffee stewed on the coals. We cooked and dined by candlelight.

Breakfast was a repeat of supper and we were milking by hand as a murky dawn crept in the barn windows. The cows were thirsty but we fed them snowy hay from the lean-to back of the barn and congratulated each other for having stored some there. That snow stopped their complaints. Back at the house the clock still said 3:25.

By nine the Crawford Electric Co-op linemen, who had been working all night against such odds as gale winds, driving snow, downed trees and blocked roads, had found and corrected our troubles. I washed dishes, made fresh coffee and listened to cancellations on the radio. The Boss got the barn cleaned, the drive scraped out and we were ready for the snowplow.

It wasn't easy, all that milking by hand when we hadn't done it for years. And according to the facts, I worked harder than he did. I milked eight cows to his seven. But just to show you how misleading facts and statistics can be, I milked all the easy cows and left the hard ones for him. He didn't notice that. If only I could keep my mouth shut. Or stay away from the typewriter.

⟶ ·

Headline 1974—Depression Looms

Who is this scratching at our door?
It seems we've seen that face before.
Four decades haven't changed him much,
He's peevish, snarling, sly and such.
But fear is not too sharp a pang
Though he be lean and sharp of fang.
Should Fate decree that we be et
At least it's by someone we've met.

⟶ ·

Kidspeak: If honeybees make honey do bumblebees make bumbles?

⟶ ·

Feline Fracases

There is a bunting order among cows and a pecking order among chickens and I don't think anybody tries to change that. Here

85

in the barn there is a cuffing order among cats and I am trying to buck it all the time. Of course that is only while I am in the barn. I suppose it functions constantly when I am not there.

It appears to be a matriarchy, males' nature not being so much cuffing as elimination of rivals and then too, tomcats usually shirk responsibility and any permanent family ties. All kittens are cuffed, sometimes by their mothers, just as often by another relative. All females who consider themselves permanent residents cuff each other but don't carry animosity too far, taking turns backing down.

But sometimes, as is the case here now, two will gang up on a third and drive it away. So Tiger and Gloria rule the barn while Lynn sneaks in for a fast drink, then hurries away to wherever she calls home.

Two males, not yet ready to go out seeking their fortunes, or whatever, sit grandly on two hay bales and serenely watch the family bickering. Nobody cuffs them. Whitey is still young enough to be silly and no male threat but Ted takes a benevolent bachelor uncle interest in the kittens, dragging in an occasional mouse for them. He also takes an interest in any new female that tries to become part of the clan.

The two ruling queens take a different interest in those female arrivals and there is where I take a hand for their attacks are vicious. They soon learn that a milk stool will come flying through the air if the fracas gets too ugly. I worry about what goes on when I am not there but even I cannot live in the barn.

⌐▦▦⌐

Compact Chronology

My career took off and paralleled our farming life when I got a job with Glenn Hagar at the Crawford County Independent in Gays Mills. When it was sold to Ralph Goldsmith, owner of the Boscobel Dial I remained as editor for a year, then worn out from night meetings, day hours and chores, I left that and spent a couple of years just happily farming.

After the death of my mentor, Hagar, I worked with his widow, Marian, in her printing business, the Independent Press. No longer needed there, I got a job at NCR Corporation in Viroqua as printer and linotype operator. Bought out the Independent Press business. I would have bought the linotype if I had learned to repair one. Quite soon I turned that printing business over to Marjie, who still runs it. Laddie died. And at this point we were preparing for an auction and retirement from farming.

⌐▦▦⌐

There Is No Funny Way To Say Goodbye

How do you say goodbye to a cow? If she has been a kicker, a bunter, a producer with poor returns, any way that you say it is good enough. Years ago we had a dairy-dropout we decided to send to the locker. First she tried to kill those helping load her into the truck. Then she jumped over the rack, down over the hood (Scout's honor) and ran back in the barn. Some time later we were eating her with relish and maybe a little ketchup.

But by the time you are ready to quit farming you have been culling for years and all have become good friends. Yes, the date has been set. February 1. And no, we are not selling the farm. There is no place we would rather live unless I could build a house out in the woods. And he won't let me.

Chore time is strange. We thought we had it planned so all would be dry at sale date. But a couple fouled us up so now we have to go out, put the milkers together, milk Georgie and Kathy, plus Isabel at night and half a dozen strippers in the morning. Takes longer to clean up than to milk.

If sale day turns out to be what is called "farm auction weather," snowy and cold, come in the house to say hello, get warm, have coffee. The latchstring will be out and signs made by the grandchildren will show the way to kitchen, living room, wherever.

Just come in. I won't be answering the door. In fact I will be avoiding the barn side of the house. Darned if I am going to watch Rosie bewildered as they drive her out into a sale ring or whatever they do. She bewilders easy for a big girl. Over the years we have always had a Rosie and come to think of it each one was easily upset.

When you see our sale bill you may wonder about some of the things listed. I'm sure I will too because I will be at work when that is done. You don't really know what you have until you sell out or move. Probably there will be "some articles of possible antique value." And I guess they did find some stuff in that category. But we have never been antique collectors. Antique users, yes. Like Grandma Davis's spoonholder that has been on the table for 40 years. No, not for sale.

Nor is the Singer sewing machine, old when I bought it but still running the same. Sewed a lot of tobacco cloth and patched a lot of overalls. It made over children's clothes, sometimes with the child the garment was for bouncing on my knee as I treadled. Not for sale as antiques must be in good condition and this machine is in the same shape I am—decrepit but still working.

Whatever will I write about after February 1? I have been asked that. And I don't know. This has always seemed to be like a letter to a friend. And surely I will think of something to write to friends about.

Retirement is that time in a dairy farmer's life when he realizes he has finally developed a first class herd.

⟨※⟩

Auction Day

I almost made it. I almost got through auction day without a sad look back at the major part of our life. Good old friends, close kinfolk and friendly strangers filled the day with laughter and companionship. Starting with a strange, very last chore time and the calmest bunch of cats we've seen in a cat's age and ending after midnight, it was quite a day.

The hours from dawn to first arrivals ticked off my list of things to do like clockwork. Then the tempo jumped into a broken-legged bunny hop and I mentally tore up my list and threw them like confetti over my head.

A small section of the auction crowd.

There was one bad moment when someone near a window reported that the first cow to be shown had bolted into the orchard and had to be surrounded and driven back and taken out another door. I growled but nobody heard me that the girls would know there was something fishy if they were forced out a door that has been a tempting No-no all their lives.

Ours was the first farm sale in the area after quite a spell of "can't afford to keep 'em but can't afford to sell 'em" so it was bound to attract attention. And I believed the veteran sale-goers that it was one of the biggest they had ever seen. Not in stuff to sell, mind you. It was sort of a thermometer reading, a pulse-taking. And I can assure you if our sale was an indication, the farming business is still healthy.

For those who tried to get here and couldn't because of traffic jams, I'm sorry. Nobody expected so many. Cars were piled up two, sometimes three across the road both ways until people got no closer than half a mile away and nobody could leave.

It took a fast load of sand by Utica township, Sheriff Bill Fillbach, Deputy Everett Halverson, Soldiers Grove's Chief of Police and Vernon Officer Don Jefson on their police radios to open it up and get traffic moving.

At the end of the day when people began loading their purchases I avoided the windows, sat by the fire and visited. I asked one elderly man in overalls, "Have you quit farming?" and he answered, "Yeah, four times."

To be continued. After all, I am expecting a shortage of column material so I'm going to have to milk those cows for a few more.

$\longrightarrow$

Now It Can Be Told

That long sale day ended at a dance. A year before I had bought the set of drums played in the Boss's orchestra when he was a young man. My reason was that I had always wanted to play drums. So I coaxed him to set them up in one end of the room. Then I played oldtime records and drummed. Funny thing. My feet can keep time but my hands can't.

But I knew what would happen and it did. He couldn't resist showing me how and got caught at it. Jim Maybee told his father and Emmett and Herman Gander invited him to sit in with them if he ever wanted to. Before the sale I went (sneaked) over to a tavern which had a dance floor near Soldiers Grove and "bribed" the operator to hire them for the night of the auction. You know what I mean. I paid the fee they would have charged.

So all day long I knew he wasn't thinking about the long, dull, "my cows are gone" evening. He was thinking of what he liked best. Even better than fishing. Playing and watching people enjoy the music. And when dancers were slow to get on the floor he always crooked a finger at me then hissed, "Get out there and dance." That is what it took—the first couple. Maybe I should have told him sometime of my deception, but I think not.

⟨※⟩

There are several things hard to get used to after retiring from 40 years of dairy farming: not needing to get up so early, overalls that never get dirty and a mud room that smells like mud.

⟨※⟩

To Move Or Not To Move

If the barn cats make it through the rest of the winter in the cold barn they should be around to pester us all summer. Then as next winter approaches they can make their own decisions, to go or stay. Not all are waiting that long. Gloria didn't have to make a decision.

Friendly as she is, on the day of the auction she captivated a young fellow's heart and he asked if he could take her home with him. I sent her along, but not with my blessing. The blessing was mine—to see one of many cats leave for a new home.

Not that she was disliked here. It was her habit to go to a neighbor's farm to have her kittens, then drag them here and back again many times even before their eyes were open. We would see her coming up the road, the tiny bundle clutched by the neck, its butt dragging. This she went on doing until she had part of the family here, then she dragged these back. She was on the road almost every day.

When they could walk she called them to follow her on these back and forth trips. Once I rescued two which had followed her voice through mud puddles. It took a couple of bath towels to dry them off. So we are glad to see the last of Gloria. Unless we see the next of her, dragging kittens here from 15 miles away.

⟨※⟩

Nobody asks me to help take down tobacco anymore. They forget that I can out-dance all of them and outrun some. And I'm not reminding them.

⟨※⟩

We Lost A Good Neighbor

Never was there a better neighbor. He had shared this end of Stump Ridge, our lives, trials and triumphs since we moved up from the valley years ago. I still catch myself watching for his form, gaunt and weather-beaten as his old farm buildings, silhouetted against the sky. Each day had to end well if it began with an uplifted arm and

"Hoo-hoo" drifting over. Even if the wind was wrong we knew the call was uttered, probably mystifying someone farther east.

He was a humble man. To have told Pete how great he was would have made him snort, "Great men don't go barefoot and steal their neighbors' radishes." And it would have done me no good to try to change his thinking. He was a man set in his ways.

They were good ways. For above all he was a compassionate man. Should his neighbors' cows get into a cornfield he worried more about the cows than he did about the corn. Generous with his help, he walked far to give it, then stayed until a trouble ended. More than one evening we hurried hauling hay ahead of rain and suddenly he was there to help.

A sometimes gloomy, pessimistic man, Pete was a laugher, too. There was the time his dog Jack and our Laddie overtook a squirrel

Great-granddaughter Jessica steps out. Daughter of Kristi and Shane Deaver.

between the corncrib and the oak tree. Alerted as I cleared the supper table by their noisy dispute over who had the right to kill it, I ran with a fragile pickle dish in my hand and stopped Laddie in his tracks with one command.

Not an obedient dog, Jack ignored me. As he reached open-mouthed for the squirrel I threw and caught him squarely in the forehead with the pickle dish. Unhurt but dumbfounded, Jack turned and walked away, shaking fragments from his face. Ever after Pete laughed at the memory, "By golly, that was the end of Pearl's pickle dish."

Everything in nature received its proper awe from him. An autumn trip had him on the edge of the car seat as he spared no adjective for the beauty of forest after forest. Blackbirds exasperated him with their scolding but one evening after the nesting season had ended he walked over carrying an empty nest that had been built in a tangle of hay stems. He had been alerted to it by upset blackbirds and left that spot in the middle of his hay field unmowed.

He was a skeptical man, much of his doubting aimed at women's abilities. And his skepticism was often my spur. Hunkered down against a tree—he preferred his heels to a chair—near the hole where I was laying up rock for support of the fireplace chimney I was building he doubted, "You'll never do it," So then I had to.

And again, one of the many times he came over to help me with chores while Punk was in the hospital with heart troubles, he hunkered down by the pen where I was trying to get Big Ruby's new calf to nurse. The calf was too tall, too stubborn to lower his head and determined to find food at the wrong end of his mother. Pete said, "You'll never do it."

Mad at calf, Ruby (I don't know why) and Pete, I reached under the calf, grabbed the opposite legs and threw him. He reached up and as the hungry baby slurped and gulped, Pete went back to feeding the cows shaking his head and muttering, "Women."

He was a handyman. When a pair of cedar waxwing babies fell from their nest in the yard and we couldn't find their nest to return them to it, we took them in and fed them. When they feathered out he came carrying a huge screened cage with a perch and swing that he had built. "So they can learn to fly without messing up your house," he said.

He watched them grow and worried with me when I turned them loose in an elderberry patch near his place. Neighbor. When you lose such a one part of your own life is forever gone.

Where Are You, Barb?

"I crawled in Laddie's old dog house.
I didn't tell my brother.
For one, it is a perfect fit."
Her Grandma had another.

Gone Fishin'

A couple of weeks ago I ripped the mantel off the fireplace. It was a hickory slab that had warped in a curve and I was tired of explaining. Then I ripped a couple of boards off the old calf shelter. Maybe I should mention that the Boss was gone fishing at the time. Before he got home I had them sawed, nailed together and in place. A nice job even if I do have to say it myself.

Someone wrote to suggest that since we no longer have cows doing exciting things to write about, "Tell us what your old man is doing with his leisure time." So here you are: fishing only half as much as he expected, working twice as hard as he planned, and watching his old woman, usually with a worried look on his face.

Barn Swallows

We really have a feud going now. I will give details, then you can go ahead and take sides. It has to do with friendliness, compassion, all those positive, warm traits. That's my side.

Every summer in our busy barn we had at least one family of swallows with a nest right over our heads. Some parents tweaked us in anger, others were so congenial I got pictures of the young ones hanging onto the edges of the nest exercising their wings in preparation for flying. And I have one shot of six babies in a row on a rafter.

I thought they built above us because Mother Nature told them that they are barn swallows so go build in a barn. I was wrong. She must have told them to build their nests near people because they have followed us and are trying to put a nest above the dining room window. I say that's devotion. He says it's a mess.

They have spent three days trying to make little dabs of plaster stick to the window ledge or sitting on the electric lines discussing it. I have managed to convince him that we should at least let them try so maybe I have won. Also I have lost. He says if they are successful I have to clean up the mess.

Old Dogs and New Tricks

He's tricky, that man of mine. What man isn't, you ask? But I can see through him. What woman can't, of her own? See, many years ago he made the rule that whoever catches fish has to clean them. It has probably been 40 years since I wet a hook.

Now that we have a boat his plan is that when I get home from work we will grab a lunch, boat, bait and take off for the Mississippi. There we will be out on the river watching the sun go down, the moon come up saying, "Just think, we don't have to hurry home and milk cows." I know he is figuring that I will catch fish and thus have to clean them. I'm tricky, too. I won't bait my hook.

All you people worrying about aging—don't. You probably wonder if life really does begin at 40 like they say. Let me reassure you. It doesn't. It begins at 60. Now that the Boss is playing for dances I am dancing. And I just learned to polka. If only I had learned it while I could still make it once around the floor.

I'm Ready—Almost

In preparation for launching the Ark—our new fishing boat—cowardly me bought a life jacket. No cheapy. It's first class, four digits on the cash register with a decimal point half way, guaranteed to last a lifetime and keep me afloat to Hawaii and back.

I didn't believe it. So I jumped in the creek. Dressed appropriately, of course—bathing suit and first class life jacket. Logically two pounds should not support 130, both objects soaking wet, but they did. And it was fun paddling around pretending that I could swim. I'm not sure I will be so filled with glee when it is the big Mississippi River that I'm floating in.

We're Old

As if we really needed any proof of our aging—all the grandchildren have outgrown the swing set that we installed under the trees back in diaper days. Seems all they use it for now is to get attention. And they do: "You're too big . . . don't swing so high . . . it's tipping over . . . that slide wasn't made for running up and down on . . . eek."

More Chickens?

You are just going to have to let me raise some chickens again, I said, what with the present price of eggs. He said Hmph and I said don't you remember that nice little yellow hen we had once and how she always came into the kitchen to eat lunch with us. See, here's her picture standing by the table and I'm feeding her something. I'm not sure what. Probably not a chicken sandwich.

Remember she wouldn't lay her egg anywhere but in the wood box behind the cookstove. Bless her heart, she would stand on the porch all morning, holding it I suppose, until somebody opened the door, then she would zip in, jump in the wood box and rustle around in the bark and chips in the corner, then come dashing out wild-eyed and we had to be ready to open the door so she could hurry out to cackle while the enthusiasm of production, or whatever they cackle for, was affecting her. Remember? I guess maybe he does. That's why he won't let me have chickens again.

Our daughter insisted on picking and snapping string beans. It was the Fourth of July and we were having a picnic. Where did I go wrong?

Recruiting Labor

When Marjie and I began rejuvenating the granary for a summer guest house we had the "I want to do it myself" attitude. But as time went by there were jobs we simply needed more brawn for than we had between us. Then I resorted to finagling. After all, I didn't want to come right out and say we couldn't do it.

Take building a doorstep. I knew I would need a lot of rocks to fill the form before I mixed cement so I asked him, "Should they be smaller than a bread box? Bigger than a baseball? Like this? Or this?" I was showing sizes with my hands as he always did when describing a fish that got away.

In disgust he said, "Come on. I'd better help you or you will get it all wrong." There's really nothing like a show of stupidity for getting a man to help you without asking him. But you men have got to give me credit for this—I waited until the ballgame was over. I bet if he were to run for office he would be elected on your sympathy vote alone.

Advice to brides on how to keep a husband, if not content, at least quiet when you goof. Get a bigger goof on him, and it is reasonably sure you will unless, heaven forbid, you married a perfect man. At our house if the conversation gets around to my latest, or any, rhubarb, I jump in and bring up one of his. In football that's called interception.

A Vacation—Finally

A vacation away from it sure makes the home farm look good. And I'm one of those people whose internal bubbles and butterflies prevent life anywhere from becoming dull. Frightening now and then, never dull. Like finding how pleasant it is driving a freeway and then suddenly finding yourself on the Duluth-Superior bridge, screaming, "but I wasn't planning on being behind the wheel when we hit the bridge" and no way to change drivers and the butterflies busted the bubbles.

But let's start the travelogue at the beginning. I promise it will be only the highlights and maybe a few lowlights. Waysides are such pleasant places to stretch your legs. Right? We stopped at a couple, looked at streams and rocks and then I spied one that I was sure was ocean bottom shell conglomerate. It wasn't but I did spy some bees so left quickly. Unbeknownst I picked up a passenger that stung me near Grand Meadow, Minn.

Then there was the two-hour traffic jam approaching Farm Fest. During the inch at a time driving we got acquainted with some FFA boys in a car in one of the other two lanes. When we drew closer and could see the fest grounds were a sea of mud from heavy rain the day before I hopped out of our car, ran up to theirs and gave them our tickets. Then we left the pack at the gate and headed north.

Lake Superior turned out to be too cold, too rough, too scary for me but it was really blue and I guess one out of four ain't bad. Seasoned travelers may laugh at one thing that really bothered me. It looked like where the lake and the horizon met the water curved up and was higher than the land on which I stood. And I can't swim.

We saw many things to wonder about. Up ahead along the highway at the top of the state there was a large black bird. I decided it was an obese crow. It was not afraid at all and stayed on the shoulder as we drove past. Later friends told us it was a raven. Our first. Then we bought our first cranberries right out of the marsh.

Most streams were almost dry and we were amazed at the deep red color of some of them in the north. Iron, I suppose. Or rust. Even lakes were just huge mud puddles and driving alongside one the boss said, "There's some driftwood if you want to go out there and get it." The surface appeared almost dry but very treacherous so I declined.

Along the Spirit River later a friend helped me find some pretty driftwood and rocks and it prompted the Boss to protest my taking them home and I said, "Sticks and stones may break my bones but not after I get them into a lawn arrangement." After my vacation was over

Punk said he caught fish because he thought like a fish.

and I was back at work I was asked, "Did you get a lot of cleaning and canning done?" Couldn't think of a thing to say except "No, was I supposed to?"

— ✺ —

Morning Alarm

Ordinarily I wake up in the morning as fresh as a pet hamster at midnight. But that 5 a.m. caught me with my eyes still shut and I went through the whole ritual of cooking, eating and getting ready to go to work without knowing it. Packed my brown bag lunch and started bleary-eyed out the ridge, yawning and groaning. Turned on the heater as it was a nippy morning. Rounded a corner and startled a skunk. Didn't kill him, mind you, but suddenly I was wide awake. You just can't beat a startled skunk for snapping you to attention.

— ✺ —

Degrees of Courage

The farm was getting pretty boring for the grandchildren so I took them to the barn, now empty of cows, where hay bales still half fill the mow and the lean-to behind it. Sure enough, there within reaching distance of a beam hung a hay rope, securely tied to the pulley, which was wedged into place on the track.

As a child I was a swinger so it was natural to grasp the rope. But as an adult I have gotten a fear of height and wasn't able to push off from the beam, swing out and drop. I relinquished the rope and moved over on the beam.

Al swung out, cleared the closed hay chute structure in front of us and dropped into soft broken hay bales. That swinging rope added to my idea of the height so I carefullly stepped over onto the chute frame, jumped and fell sprawling in the hay.

Barb then grasped the rope and swung way out. But instead of dropping into the hay she screamed and swung back onto the beam. Her hang-up was the drop. So there we were playing together, taking turns—Al swinging, letting go and jumping; me just jumping; Barb swinging, screaming, not jumping. In disgust 10-year-old Al said, "If I could put you two together I would have one good partner."

— ✺ —

Now and then I sputter to the man on my right about the driving habits of others. Quite often I include blistering language. But only once did the MOMR comment on mine. He said, "You rounded that corner too fast." Humbly I replied, "I know it." Loose gravel and I did know it.

He's Retired

The Boss and I play pool every day when I get home from work. He beats me every game but one. I guess that's because he is so glad to see me that he stands across the table from me and points out just where I should hit my ball to bank or drop it direct. "Just kiss it," he says. Then I beat him. But after that I have to use my own judgement and it ain't good.

Happy Days Are Here Again

Here you have one happy woman. The empty barn—our deserted, bedraggled, miserable, ready-to-begin-falling-down barn has cows in it. And suddenly it looks like a lady after a face lift—young, perky, years of life left.

Our neighbors—Ed, Pat, Dave and Teresa—were in need of better housing for their cows as winter approached. And you know how easy it is to build nowadays. So we have rented them our barn. Thank goodness I was at work the day they put the cows in. I was also at work the day before, when they tried to. I've had my full share of trying to convince a cow she should go where she doesn't want to.

So it was an accomplished fact when I came home and found the barn with that old familiar lived-in look. For a while I was content to just visit with them (the cows I mean) when I went out to feed the cats. I haven't yet asked for their names so I can address them familiarly, but I will.

Then one evening when our neighbors drove up to do that final feeding and bedding down, the idea came to me. In the interests of saving gas they can stay home and I will make that goodnight trip since it is just a short walk for me. The chore fills a void in my life but it is a little disconcerting to walk into the house every night to the same greeting: "Phew!"

At the NCR printing plant where I work I sometimes find that each job requires a different color ink. So a lot of time is spent washing one color off the press and putting another color on. Old printers never die, they just get washed up.

The Good Life

It's great, life is, two ways. I still work, get a paycheck so have my own money to spend and go dancing every Saturday night until one. Punk plays the drums with a couple of orchestras. I do the driving, carry the drums and dance.

About his music-making. He played with the local orchestra when he was young but as our farm chores multiplied he had to give it up. In those years his instrument was the accordion and now that he has quit farming I suggested that he buy another as the first had simply worn out. He insisted that his fingers were too stiff for playing. So I sneaked and bought him one.

Little by little he began playing, delighted to find that he still could. Then one day he said he was going to buy a different one and when I asked why he said the one I had bought was a woman's. I didn't know accordions had a gender. When he brought the new one home I understood. The keys were wider.

From then on I have had two kinds of music in the house any time of day or evening—accordion melodies (and he knows so many and plays by ear) and his drum accompaniment to oldtime records. I never get enough.

Retirement Hazards

Hey girls, when your husband retires you may find it a mixed blessing. I do have help with the dishes now but when he dries the pots and pans he has to cross the kitchen behind me to put them away in the stove drawer.

A long-handled pan must be tempting and he always whacks my rear with it as he goes by. He claims that is his right. I am going to get out our marriage certificate and study the fine print. Anyway, now that I have warned you there is time for you to remodel your kitchen. The best way to handle temptation is to remove it.

Being the oldest worker in a plant where everyone else ranges from younger to much younger I should be a little despondent about my old age. But it's hard, almost impossible, when the young man working beside me calls me "Pearl, Baby." How can I retire and leave that to go home where I'm just Grandma?

Visiting the Social Security office to register for retirement Medicare is for the elderly like the very first day of school for the young. You don't feel you really belong there but there isn't much you can do about it.

My retirement and our wedding anniversary come about the same time so we are celebrating. First time ever for our anniversary—we have always been stripping tobacco on that date. Think of it—45 years married to the same person. Surprising that it has endured so long—a bossy, opinionated, egotistical despot married to an angel. Tsk. Tsk.

Twelve Days Of Retirement

On the first day of retirement my true love said to me, "Now that you are home for good you can take over some of our chores." On the second day of retirement my TL said, "As long as you are going out to feed the birds you can take out the garbage." Old Auntie's ghost whispered "Don't you remember I told you never to start anything you don't want to keep on doing." I reminded her I wasn't starting, just taking up where I left off.

On the third day I said, "As long as I am no longer holding down a full-time job you don't need to help with the dishes." So my TL didn't, darn him. On the fourth and fifth days he said, "Don't walk in front of the TV."

Then there were the sixth and seventh days stripping tobacco a couple of places just to keep our hands in and also I dived into a messy corner of the basement where junk had been accumulating since the house was built and on the eighth day I sent my TL to the dump. What a satisfying job, to shuck off rubbish. Wonder if rich people know that pleasure.

The ninth began mild and we went at a dirty job—cleaning the chimney. It wasn't fun. He was on the roof because I am afraid of height, I was in the basement getting a face full of soot. A chain tied together is pulled up and down by a length of binder twine to scrape creosote off the walls of the chimney. The twine broke.

You wouldn't expect a plumber's rat to rescue a chimney sweep, would you? He cranked the auger down, it snagged into the rope and he pulled the whole thing to the top. After that it was scrape and carry and we finished just as it started to snow.

On the tenth day, nursing sore knuckles, I realized a working days' dream. I sat in the window, with my TL, and watched snow drift the roads shut and listened to school closings. I got a book and a cup of coffee and my nostalgia—missing work and friends—began to fade.

On the eleventh day my true love said to me, "Since you aren't doing anything you could patch a couple pairs of overalls for me." So I got out the sewing machine that was older than I was when I bought it after we were married. Then I read another book.

On the 12th day I got out of my rocking chair and said to my TL, "Let's do something with this retirement. I've dragged my feet because I want the ice on the river at least three feet thick before I go fishing. Let's at least go look at the river." So we did. And in 15 miles we only saw one fisherman and he was going home.

Dorothy with her charges at Bethel House in Viroqua, where she has worked since retiring from NCR Corporation.

A Dog Story

I buried the puppy quickly. The day was chilly and the wind whipped fading leaves around the house to gather in the lee of a shrub. I started at his tail, a black tail with a white tip at the end. It had wagged a lot since her owner, whoever it was, dumped her near our farm and we found her sitting on the porch looking at us with belonging in her eyes.

Then I covered the body, almost all black, and her feet, each one white with black speckles. The snowy white chest still showed so I covered that, then last but very quickly I covered the head. The reason I had to start at the tail and work fast, leaving her head until last was because the instant her head was covered the small furry body shot out of the pile of leaves, pounced into another pile and waited for me to do it all over again.

Life on the farm with another dog is nothing like past experiences that many other dogs, all dumped, brought us. The main reason we are in such a muddle—sometimes glee, sometimes aggravation—we have never had a dog still in kindergarten.

Boots

There was an old lady whose pet pup
Was so peppy it always was hepped up
Its smiling jaws nipped her
Its frolicking tripped her
Her aging has been somewhat stepped up.

An Un-foolish Man

We lost another neighbor and good friend. Odin Larson came to this country from Norway as a young man. Old and retired he shared Pete Eide's house, living in half with a door to shut between. We learned to know him sitting on our lawn summers, playing cards at his kitchen table winter nights. He shared Pete's tobacco work, too. I sat on the planter with him and he planted his own and those I missed. We began spearing together and he left me way behind. Once long ago he had fallen in a shed and was left with a deformed hip, painful, I'm sure, but he was a man who never complained.

His almost every comment began with "Ya" said with a rising inflection. We took him and Pete on an autumn color drive and while Pete and I raved about the scene he said, "Ya, foolishness—it's only trees." We took them to see slides of his native Norway and on the way home I asked if he liked them.

"Ya," he said, "but that's not Norway." His home was above the Arctic Circle and they often had seen herds of thousands of reindeer.

On his birthday we took a three-layer cake over one snowy night, Punk lit a candle on it and we went in singing, "Happy birthday to you..." He said,

"Ya, that's the first birthday cake I ever had."

Life got easier after he put himself in the Soldiers Grove nursing home. Nobody had ever cared for him before. After a trip to the hospital he told me with a happy smile, "Ya, it's good to be home." And when he learned his illness was terminal he told us with a chuckle, "Ya, I almost made it to 90."

At his funeral there were the minister, undertaker, pallbearers, the women serving lunch, Punk and me. He had no kith nor kin. Had I mourned to him about that he would have chuckled and said, "Ya, such foolishness."

Time gallops on. Our little great-granddaughter is being potty trained. Her mother tells me she insists the pot is for wearing on her head. After all, it fits.

Card Champ

Everybody is aware of the importance of February 14 and the lucky so-and-so whose birthday is on that day gets so many cards they go to his head. I consider hiding some when I go to get the mail. My birthday is right after his and again he can say, "You won't get as many as I did." He's right. After all, who forgets a Valentine person. And who remembers one whose day was commemorated by discovery of the TB bacillus?

Hillside Roleo

We are putting up next year's wood supply. The trees were felled last fall. They had been marked by the forester as part of the woodland conservation program and they are all on a hillside on our land with a road below.

Using the chain saw, he stands with one leg lower, the other above with the knee bent. I, the go-fer below him, pull away and stack the brush, going along the hillside with a hitch in my git-along. I guide the chunks to the road side as they roll down from his saw. How much easier this would be if we were short-legged on one side.

My life is just full of excitement. The Boss taught me how to catch night crawlers. At first I yelled, "I see one all the way out," and grabbed for it. Then I took to whispering it. I soon learned there is no such thing as a night crawler half way out.

Excitement In The Guest House

The granary guest house that Marjie and I remodeled during two summers has been abandoned. The last family visiting here came screaming to the house in the middle of the night: "Bats!" They spent the rest of the night distributed between one bed and pallets on the floor.

A few days later I got the neighbors' boy to climb our extension ladder and tap small pieces of wood that I had prepared into the spaces between roof boards. We worked hard trying to fill every opening as big as a quarter which I had been told was the smallest space that a bat could squeeze through.

Several weeks later a grandson and five of his pals spent the weekend out there. In the morning we asked how their night had been. "Great!' they said." When the bats came out and started flying around we used the badminton rackets." Fear or fun—it's all in the point of view.

⸺⫘⫘⫘⟶ -

A Visit To Vernon Memorial

The Boss came home from his favorite hospital and the house changed from a way station where I came briefly to change clothes, feed and let Boots in or out, into a home again. Boots came alive. She is his dog, just tolerates me, lets me open doors, things like that. A normally silent dog, when he got home she either welcomed him home or scolded him for being gone.

The family wouldn't let me ski while I was alone. "We don't want you both in the hospital," they said. So the day after he came home I went out across the field from the house where he could watch from a window and if I fell and signalled a broken leg he could call for help.

What he said was that he would call the one with a snowmobile and have him drag me home behind it. There was also some talk of the tractor and spreader or front end loader so I was careful.

I asked if he had good care in the hospital and did he often need to use the calling for help button. Said he never did. Nurses, aides, even maintenance workers were constantly popping in to see if he wanted anything. I've had little experience in hospitals (how old are you, son?) but when I do that's where I'm going, too.

While he was there the heart specialist made a regular call from La Crosse and stopped in to visit. So we had a chance to ask a question that had worried us. Should Punk give up playing his accordion? The doctor fairly snorted, "Of course not. Play just as much as you feel like— do you want to turn into an old toad?"

⸺⫘⫘⫘⟶ -

A Dash of Caution

When we go to entertain at nursing homes I don't take part, having the musical ability of a one-handed frog with a cold. I carry the instruments and dance with anyone who wants to. Last time one new resident sent an aide over to ask if I would dance with her. She stood up shaky but game and kept perfect time as we waltzed around the floor. Finally she said, "I'd better quit. It's fun but I have a pacemaker and I don't want to overload it." Grit with a dash of caution.

The computer Marjie uses for the newspapers Boscobel Dial and Independent-Scout is next to her antique printing press.

Me Dummy—You Happy

All I said was if you are going to stand there and wait for me to hang my head in shame better pull up a chair and rest your feet because women have just as much right to do dumb things as men and I said that because he had just asked me where was my jacket and I said I forgot it and he said I just knew you would and I said big deal and he said but twice in one day and I said well that takes practice and it had because we went to Boscobel where he and Emmett Maybee played for senior citizens (I just go along to carry the drums) and it wasn't raining when we left so I forgot my coat and when we got to Gays Mills and he let me out at a meeting it was so he lent me his jacket and when I left there the sun was shining so of course I didn't need a jacket and I forgot it and he's been telling everybody about it since. It doesn't take much to keep a husband happy.

Minority Groups

For every woman who says, "It Goes without saying,"
Then lets it
There's a man who catches the biggest of fish
And forgets it.

~⬦~

Back To The River

The Boss got an OK from his doctor to go fishing again. I don't know how the IRS would rate that but to our local banker, a twice a day fisherman himself, it's a capital gain.

So we went to the river for the first time in ages. We caught one walleye, one cold, one wood tick; saw two barges and waves too high for anything but a barge; a flock of ducks too far away to recognize and one heron; lost one hook in the rocks and two in a tree. He tried again to teach me how to fish and without trying I taught him again how not to.

I got one wet foot, snagged 27 times, hungry five times. While I had a few hours to think—and except for getting un-snagged what else did I have to do—I put two and any other number together and got the answer to my fishing trips. I carry bait pail, gear pail, lunch and net. Hey, even better than catching fish it's nice to be needed.

~⬦~

Old Folks—New Tricks

Unlike old dogs, some old folks can learn new tricks. But it ain't easy. I never planned on learning to run our big new riding lawnmower, it being just a shade smaller than a tractor, but while the Boss was in the hospital this time I had to.

A grandson mowed it once then school started and the grass wouldn't wait for the weekend. Our yard matches the mower or I would have used the push one. I also learned to start the big rider. And that isn't easy. I have to lay a screwdriver, the metal part, between two thingamajigs. I also learned not to touch the tip of the screwdriver right away.

~⬦~

Have you seen the latest fashion for women? I have. They show dizzying kaleidescopes of shapely, lovely young models cavorting in wildly hued jump suits. With such luscious dressing to be had—oh, to be in my salad days again.

~⬦~

Horrified Husband

I have this trait which has upset my husband for most of our married life, or at least for the years that I was earning money. If I have any I spend it. His reactions range from horror to indignation, to scolding for my extravagance and back to horror. Then I bought something that really blew it. And I thought—well, our marriage will go out in a blaze of something.

One afternoon while I was busy he disappeared. I didn't wonder where he was although when he went for a walk Boots always went with him and now she was here listening to the radio he always has on while I ironed. I went to the sink for a drink of water and saw him almost over to Pete's, perched on my tiny new moped. He went out of sight and came home later from visiting the neighbors, putzing along with a big smile on his face. Horror doesn't stand a chance against fun.

⸻

The surest sign of a successful big weekend family gathering on the farm—the pump held up and the sewer didn't give out.

⸻

Walking The Fence

Fencing is not the pure unadulterated fun that propaganda had me believing. There's heat, especially when wearing high rubber boots, there are weeds as high as the boots and there are deer flies.

What happened, the Boss came home from fishing and nonchalantly said that the electric fence was not firing good enough. Nonchalantly is the way a husband who knows you have a dozen things to do announces that you have one more. To keep the stock in the valley pasture he wants the fence firing fiercely. The way I usually find out it isn't is when I don't bend low enough when I crawl under.

Ordinarily I would have enjoyed the walk. If I had remembered to put on a long sleeved shirt. If I had bought a new can of insect repellent. If I hadn't planned on baking a rhubarb pie with a latticed top crust and was going to have to study weaving directions. There wasn't time when I got back and no, I didn't weave it right.

There was one thing going for me. Our company was a couple of temporary bachelors who were hungry enough to not care about the woven top crust, didn't notice I hadn't dusted and offered to do the dishes. Finally, I did not find the short in the fence and will have to go back and look again before the stock gets out. And I found out that fencing is adulterated. And not necessarily fun.

⸻

Language Lessons

For the last half year the Boss has been trying to teach Boots and me some Norwegian. She is learning. I'm not. All day she follows him as he works on his fishing boat and gear, to the garden, gets the mail.

She is waiting for the one sentence she knows best and likes best. He tells me—and her—slowly, and this is spelled phonetically, "Skalve lisapaw in liten choia?" She races to the Scout and jumps up and down waiting for him to open the door.

Back through the fields they ride, along the fence where they can see into the woods and down to the pond where ducks are nesting. All the nut trees are loaded, deer have left tracks in the bare ground along the edge of the cornfield and one maple tree is a blaze of color. Maybe I would get to go for a ride if I could learn Norwegian.

Bees!

Every summer it's the same. Bees of any variety are starting a family. No, a nation. And every summer that building site is right where I simply have to walk or work. And I spend an awful lot of time thinking of a means of getting rid of them that won't get me stung.

Like several weeks of mental torture before the middle of a hot July night when I stood almost under a basketball-sized hanging nest in the chickenhouse, dressed in the boss's ice fishing coveralls with the collar tucked under a tight winter cap, earflaps down. I eliminated the whole hive with only one casualty—a near nervous breakdown.

Nobody else gets excited about bees. I've heard enough "Don't bother them and they won't bother you" to last a lifetime. The problem is my imagination. One of the children might blunder onto the nest or appear to be a menace to the bees. Or this time the Boss might be stung more than twice and two times was enough to make him deathly sick.

As fatally allergic to bee stings as he probably is, he is not afraid of them. I, who only get a little itchy swelling, am petrified but not to the point that I can't run, wave my arms and scream. So to save him from his rash courage and me from death by fright I am going to have to take myself in hand and go at them with a can of spray, a pingpong paddle and a clear line of escape.

This particular menace is a colony of bumblebees increasing in size above my cases of type and paper cutter. The reason they can be there is because when Uncle Carl was ordered to build a milk house, as every farmer was back then, he enclosed a corner of the garage. Since then we built one attached to the remodeled barn and tore out these side walls, leaving the ceiling with a layer of insulation intact. That's where they are.

My first warning was when some huge bumblebees zoomed past my ear in early spring. Now all day long we see smaller, growing bees, going in and out. If I got no printing jobs until winter, or if I didn't need the car I would be alright. So a dark night, a climb up a stepladder, a whole can of bee killer, another near nervous breakdown and they are done for. Man, do I love winters.

Jim, with one of his trucks that he uses for hauling forms, operates a concrete business out of Cottage Grove.

First Camping Trip

For the first time ever we are about to go camping. Not your basic sleep on the ground, build a cooking fire (unless we do that for fun), bathe in the river camping, but to a couple of novices this will be rugged enough. You don't think so? I have never pulled anything behind a vehicle I was driving on a highway. Rugged, especially for one passenger.

Remembering that song, "Give me 40 acres and I'll turn this rig around," I took six miles and did just fine. We went out our ridge pulling our "new" camper, along a highway about a mile, then back around on another side road and back up the hill. Chickens didn't actually fly squawking out of my way but there were a few wary looking dogs as we passed by.

⌐⫸ -

When the Boss said he had confidence in my ability to get us to the river and back we began choosing the right days. We almost picked July 6, which would have put us on the river bank during that bad storm. As it was, when we get back day after tomorrow I am going to have to go to work with saw, axe and snaking rope. Parts of three trees went down— on the lawn of course.

⌐⫸ -

The most important things that old people should do—stay as well as we can and have as much fun as we can.

⌐⫸ -

Fun—Fun—Fun

Think of it. Two old farmers, each one three score and then some, going on an adventure that ten, even 20 years ago would have seemed an impossible dream. A good time? After we got to Blackhawk Park without being hit by a train as we crossed the railroad tracks, I parked the outfit. A little later I pulled it out and parked it under a better shade tree. The third time I wondered if that was a good place he moved it and said, "Now leave it there."

This camping is a whole new wonderful world. No telephone. I carried my coffee down to the river bank. He fished steadily and caught a lot. I caught one. Two house boats anchored for the night and a dozen people harmonized old songs through the evening.

I think heaven on earth is a river bank in the summertime. Did he get as ecstatic as I did? He's a taciturn Norwegian. But I did hear him tell someone, "We'll be back." I will settle for that. The cost was well worth it.

⌐⫸ -

Serendipity

It will be great to celebrate our fifty-first wedding anniversary this year. Last year he was in the hospital. Besides being back to playing pool, wielding the lefse stick and taking Boots for walks and rides, he got out and did a lot of those fall chores wives don't always think of.

I am finally getting our fleas under control after a traumatic day when I took Boots down out in the yard and powdered her black coat white. It was a sunny day but we made a cloud that had us both sneezing. She ran away and stayed all day but came home minus the powder and some fleas. So I'm happy.

The new submersible pump works like a dream. It must. We aren't aware it is and we do have water. No more pump jack throwing a belt, no well pipe freezing this winter. The Boss is playing accordion again at senior citizen doings and nursing homes. He and Alfred Nedrelo do a lot of it. They rode a trailer in the Apple Festival—motorized music—and when he isn't feeling well Alfred comes and they play a while, then he rests a while. So he's happy, too.

When I Am Old

When I am an old woman I shall wear red, but only for dress-up. Mostly I will wear blue jeans because I may need to climb through a barbed wire fence. Or climb a tree.

I shall walk my dog at midnight when we can't sleep. And go out barefoot in winter if I want to. And do all the things grownups said I must not do because "you will catch cold or it will make you sick." And I shall spend my Social Security on playthings that will bring the young to see my playthings. And me.

I shall bake cookies and share them with my dog because some of my best friends are dogs and what are cookies for but to share with friends. And learn to square dance. I needn't prepare my friends for what I will do because they are used to such.

I know it because my husband once said, "Nothing you do surprises me anymore." Wow. But I shall never wear purple because when I was a child all the old women wore purple. Or black. Maybe it was the law.

And Then He Was Gone

I didn't expect to come back to writing this soon, if ever. But I had to. There is something you should know and you might not find it out except from me.

Scan the magazines on any rack and there will be at least one front cover blurb urging you to read its story about coping with grief. There are even books about it. And in a year and a half of constant worry, I was aware of them all.

Most stress the importance of deep sadness—the crying. They state the family must allow it, bear with it and not make an effort to bring the grieving one out of it until that person is ready. Don't say,

"Come on now, knock it off, be cheerful." Deep grief must run its course. What not one of those articles said is that the course is made easier if there is laughter. Yes, laughter.

Maybe the writers consider it indelicate to mention laughter. But within an hour after my husband died the house was filled with family and friends. Never will I hesitate to go to another in the same circumstances. Their presence was balm.

There were tears. There were coffee cups and food brought and set out for those who had come without supper and didn't expect any. And then someone said, "Do you remember . . . ? and the memory was so funny. And there was laughter, shaky at first, and with it the same feeling of guilt you felt the first time you clapped in church.

And I said, "He bought my Christmas present just this morning. It will be a roll of stamps (a tradition) and probably it is still in his coat pocket." I searched. And gave up. Then I walked to the mantle and reached up to the miniature bobsled someone gave him when he was in the hospital a year ago. There under the seat were two rolls of stamps. And it was as though he reached out and said, "Gotcha." More tears. But good laughter, too.

There were two days of hazy living just on the shaky surface, then I was in the front pew where I had never sat before and I waited for the wave of panic that would come when I really comprehended all those people behind me looking at the back of my head. It didn't come. Instead such a feeling of caring enveloped me it was like a warm wave— the church was filled with it.

For years I've scoffed, with some others, at funeral services. "They are barbaric. Shouldn't be." Never will I believe that again. How else can all those people offer their sympathy? It is an intensely caring period and it eases the transition from that part of life with him, to the next without him.

In accepting sympathy I tried to follow my family's lead: "Thank you, but we had him a whole year longer than we—and he—expected and we are grateful." And that wonderful bonus year after his wise doctor discarded the drugs that kept his heart beating regularly but made the rest of his body so sick that he didn't care, and he substituted one less potent was great. In moderation he did all the things he loved— fished, camped, played accordion. The quality of his life kept improving.

So now I join the legion of women to whom grief recurs at odd and unexpected times. "No, I don't know how cold it is. He always watched the thermometer" or "The weather forecast? No, he..." I forgot to put a present out for the mail carrier and the Sunday paper deliverer. I drive to town with my gas gauge on E. I turn to tell him something and he isn't there.

A Gift To Make The Most Of

Life is a precious gift. It is meant to be lived to the fullest, not forever spent in devastating sadness. That does none any good, least of all the loving families who have to watch a life wasted.

Like a country song: "Give me one more chance—one more shot—one more day," for the grieving one left behind to refuse the need for going bravely on into the altered future is to deny the gift of life. Each life has many stages. We must accept and make the most of each one of those stages.

Many years ago the youngest of our clan, four at the time, was asked as children often are, what he was going to be when he grew up. There was a wait—silent, serious, then he said, "First I'd like to grow up."

Long before the day he bought the stamps that would have been my hidden surprise he came home with a beautifully gift-wrapped package. After Christmas I left it unopened for weeks. Unopened, it was a

Bound newspaper files were searched for the material to fill these pages.

symbol of 50 years of gifts. Finally I weakened. I had looked all over for a coffeepot that would be wide enough to cover my smallest stove burner. I never found one. If he had watched me open the package he would have gloated, "I found one."

⟨⟩

Every morning Boots and I walk over to Pete's just before daylight. I always hope to see northern lights but will settle for a meteor. So I stand tall, turning and twisting and watching the sky. If a meteor flashes across the sky I don't want to miss it. Every meteor deserves a dizzy audience of at least one.

⟨⟩

Square Dancing

Here I am in kindergarten you might say, trying to learn to square dance. It has been a longtime ambition and I must not miss a single lesson. This is a problem—my nose's keratoses had to be treated so I am an ugly sight. But I don't think the club will mind. If they can tolerate my screw-ups of the square they can tolerate my nose. Education must go on.

When I was young I danced a lot but those dances were thousands of steps, all alike, and my head got to where it didn't need to know what my feet were doing. They just did it.

Now with constantly and unexpected changes of calls at the whim of the caller my head bone doesn't seem to be connected to the foot bone in any way. And there I am lost and alone on the outside of the square, wondering if communication will ever occur.

⟨⟩

Priority

The heck with ailing annual cats.
I really don't care a lick
If each departs barn or all nine lives.
My perennial dog is sick!

⟨⟩

Ah, Winter

This time of year leans, for me, toward the plus side. There is a contentment, a serenity, pervading my days that I don't find in summer. I know there are many who suffer from depression caused by short, dark days. So much is written about the syndrome that saddens. This is incomprehensible to me, who thrives in dark, with one small pool of light.

Maybe I am closer kin to the ancient cave dwellers than others are. I am so lucky. But should SAD ever strike me I have a fast acting antidote. There is no day so sad and gloomy that the aroma of bread and cookies baking can't cure.

Elderly Abuse

I see by the papers that abuse is one of the big problems of today. And abuse of the elderly by their families is a growing part of that problem. Doesn't worry me. Let 'em abuse. I'll get even. I'm leaving them five junk drawers that haven't been cleaned nor organized for 31 years.

Happy Me

Driving out the back road last week I spied a big flock of blackbirds. Among them was one that was snow white. An albino. I was so excited that I called all my birder friends. It never takes much to make me happy. And that was a lot.

She Likes It

Once in a while someone says something nice about my column. I know because I eavesdrop a lot. I overheard one woman say to another that she likes what I write because "she makes out like she's dumb but she's not." Hey, love it. And hey, I've got one fooled.

Old age does not necessarily cause forgetfulness but it helps. When I speak to any of my family I use every name before I get to the right one. But they are all good natured about it and they will answer to anything.

Growing Old—Liking It

We owe certain things to our families, our communities and the world: to take care of our health, be uncomplaining, to have fun. So let's get at it.

Let no routine rule you. Like to sleep late? Do it. But then when you wake up way early some morning take yourself out for breakfast. Early breakfasters are friendly people. They make conversation like,

"What are you doing out so early?" Tell them the truth—you couldn't sleep. Or lie and say you are on a trip. Then go on one.

We should keep ledgers, putting the good things in our lives on one side, troubles on the other. And make sure the positive line is the longest.

⟨※⟩ ·

Whatever makes us happy we should buy if we can afford it. Don't ever say "It's probably foolish . . . my age . . . what will people say?" Enjoy. We will get mental, physical and emotional benefits and it may keep us out of the doctor's office. Take it from One Who Knows.

⟨※⟩ ·

If you can do hand stands at 70 don't quit doing them just because you are 70. Or 80.

⟨※⟩ ·

If you are still mentally alert and your daughter attends Alzheimers awareness sessions hope that she may never need her knowledge to cope with you. But give her your blessing.

⟨※⟩ ·

When your kids call attention to your advancing age with remarks like, "You shouldn't be doing that," hand back the line they used a lot when they were little and you were the one in charge: "I want to do it myself." And do it.

⟨※⟩ ·

Always be good to ourselves. Back home after a dress-up affair, shed the fancy togs and get into comfortable sweats. Dr. Dentons grown up.

⟨※⟩ ·

The breadth, the depth, the tranquility of life can be learned on a Wisconsin hilltop. And even after 81 years the anticipation of tomorrow is more exciting than ever.

117